COMPLETE HEALTHY

AIR FRYER

COOKBOOK

101 Delicious, Carefully Selected Recipes for Quick & Easy Everyday Cooking

INTRODUCTION

If you are in the market looking for an appliance that will help you to stay healthy, while at the same time allowing you to enjoy extremely delicious and mouthwatering fried foods, then the air fryer is exactly what you need!

With new, modern culinary devices being continuously invented and released into the market, few can capture the revolutionary leap that the air fryer presented when it was first launched back in 2010 by Philips. It was a significant, technological milestone that seamlessly introduced a completely new way of frying, and gave health practitioners a new perspective on fried goods.

Simply put, an air fryer is a kitchen appliance that is designed to be a multi-purpose cooking device with the capacity to fry, roast, grill and bake - all under the same hood. While Philips was essentially the pioneer who brought the appliance into the mass market, as of 2020, many more companies such as Elite, Ninja, GoWise, Nu-Wave, and a few others have entered the market with their twist on the appliance.

There are many people out there who sometimes mix up the air fryer with an 'Instant Pot', which is yet another amazing appliance, but these two appliances couldn't be more different!

Instant pots rely on the extreme build up pressure and heat to cook their meals, while air fryers use superheated air and carefully designed exhausts to evenly distribute air all around the food and cook the meal to perfection.

That being said, let's now move to the contents of this book!

If you are an absolute beginner and are looking for the perfect portal to dive into the world of air fryers, then this is the only book that you are going to need!

The introductory section of this book will cover the fundamentals of the air fryer cooking appliance and help you understand why this appliance is so awesome. I will be covering how to use the appliance, the health benefits of using the air fryer, some incredible hints andtips, and so on.

Once you are done with the intro, feel free to dive into the amazing collection of 100% handpicked and full-proof recipes that are guaranteed to make you fall in love with them.

I understand that there are hundreds of air fryer cookbooks out there in the market, but I can safely say that none of those books were written with the level of care and attention that this book has.

All of the information and recipes in this book are written after thorough research, so you can safely rely on this one with no second thought. These recipes were already produced and tried by the author himself, so you can rest easy knowing that they are the very best.

I hope that you will enjoy the contents found within this book and that it will help you to start a new and improved "Oil-Free" diet!

Bon Appetit!

**Go here to get your bonus
7-Day Meal Plan and exclusive 5-ingredient recipes
for FREE!**

Chapter 1
THE BASICS OF AN AIR FRYER

AWESOME BENEFITS OF USING AN AIR FRYER

Using the air fryer comes with a plethora of absolutely amazing health benefits that will greatly improve your cooking experience and your health in the long run! Some of the most prominent benefits include:

- The air fryer is an extremely versatile appliance that will allow you to not only air fry dishes, but also grill, roast, or even bake them as well!

- The enclosure of the air fryer is constructed by keeping the safety of its users as the top priority, and it eliminates the risk of having hot oil falling over your skin.

- The appliance is extremely easy and simple to use. The minimal use of oil results in very little build-up of debris/grease and is very seamless to clean as well.

- The pre-installed smart programs of the appliance are very carefully designed to help even amateur chefs prepare premium quality dishes.

- Since you are cooking with superheated air, the air fryer helps to save a lot of time, freeing up more of your day to spend with the people you love, and doing the things that you love.

- Using the air fryer cuts down almost 8-85% of total oil consumption, which makes it great for your heart in the long run.

- The relatively compact size and versatility of the air fryer means that you can easily install it in any corner of your kitchen (provided it has proper airflow) and free up space to keep your kitchen sleek and clean looking.

And those are just the tip of the iceberg!

BASIC STEPS OF USING THE AIR FRYER

Some people often think that using the air fryer can be a little bit daunting and difficult to some extent - the truth is far from it! Despite all of its advanced technological capabilities, the air fryer is an extremely simple and easy to use appliance making oil-free cooking a breeze.

While some of the steps will vary depending on the recipe that you are following, the core idea will always remain the same:

- For prepping your air fryer, the first step is to take out your cooking basket and drizzle a bit of oil over it.

- Place your ingredients,prepared according to the recipe instruction, into the air fryer cooking basket.

- Preheat your air fryer to the desired temperature and set the timer.

- Slide in your cooking basket once the air fryer is pre-heated, and let it cook until the timer runs out.

- Keep an eye out for recipes that ask you to shake the basket from time to time.

- Once the timer runs out, your food is ready to be served!

HOW TO KEEP YOUR FRYER CLEAN

The air fryer is possibly one of the most advanced and versatile cooking appliances to ever bless the walls of the culinary world. It helps to cook food extremely fast, requires a minimal amount of oil, and is extremely easy to use.

But just like other electrical cooking appliances, such as toasters or microwaves, air fryers also needed a good level of maintenance and cleaning to keep it running in tip-top shape for years to come.

Without regular cleaning, the appliance can accumulate dirt and debris, which might hamper the flavor of the food, produce unwanted smoke and reduce the overall quality of your prepared meal.

Regardless of what people might say, cleaning up the air fryer is actually extremely easy! All you have to do is follow the steps below:

· Start off by unplugging your air fryer from the wall socket and let it cool down. This step is extremely crucial as it will help you prevent self-injury or electrocution.

· Once your appliance has cooled down, the first thing is to clean up the pans and basket. Take out the pans, basket, baking tray and frying basket and wash them with warm soapy water. If your pan has accumulated any hard to remove debris, such as burnt batter or food, apply a bit of hot water and then wipe them off.

· Next comes the interior. For this part, you are to simply take a non-abrasive sponge/soft cloth and use hot water to clean it. First, clean the installed heating element. If there is any unwanted grease in the element, add just a small amount of dish soap to loosen it up and clean with your sponge. A good tip is to turn your appliance upside down while cleaning the heating element, as it makes it easier. Once you are done with the heating element, use your sponge to clean the interior surface. Again, if you notice any unwanted grease, simply use a bit of hot soapy water to clean it up.

· Now the exterior. Take a sponge/moist cloth and use a mild detergent to clean the external body. Make sure to refrain from using bleach or glass cleaners as they might damage the body. Alternatively, if your particular model has a stainless-steel body, then it is strongly advised that you use wipes that are specifically produced for cleaning stainless-steel structures.

Those steps should pretty much help you to keep your appliance in great shape. However, as an extended tip, it is advised that you always clean your air fryer after each of your cooking sessions to prevent dirt build up. Once you have cleaned it thoroughly, let it dry completely and make sure to store it in a clean and dry place.

AIR FRYER HEALTHY EATING TIPS

While the air fryer itself is already a healthy appliance due to the amount of oil it eliminates from your diet, there are certain tips that you can follow to make your meals even healthier!

- While the air fryer doesn't necessarily require you to add oil, some heavier recipes do require you to add/spray a small amount. Try to opt for healthier options, such as olive oil, and spray the oil after the food has been transferred to the cooking basket.

- Some people often think that food can be cooked directly in the air fryer, however, it is highly recommended that you always pre-heat your air fryer to your desired temperature 3 minutes prior to cooking. This not only helps to cook foods evenly but also ensures that your meats/veggies are not left raw and are nicely cookedwith all the nutrition intact.

- Some meat/ingredients have the tendency to stick themselves to the surface of the cooking basket while cooking. This not only makes them more prone to getting burned but might result in overcooking as well. A good and healthier way to avoid this is to carefully grease the cooking basket with healthy oils before layering your ingredients on top.

- The air fryer does not come with a built-in thermometer that you can use to accurately measure the temperature of the ingredients that you are cooking. Having a high-quality quick read thermometer will allow you to check the temperature of your meat/vegetables and ensure that they are just right. This is extremely helpful when cooking steak as a lot of the flavor and texture of the meat depends on the internal temperature. But even if you are not cooking steak, it is still important to keep the internal temperature in check to confirm that your food has been cooked properly and thoroughly. Raw or undercooked food often contains germs and bacteria that may lead to food poisoning and other complications.

- This is a very common early mistake that many users seem to make. Make sure to never overcrowd the cooking basket with excess ingredients! It will once again result in uneven cooking/crisping/browning and end up producing meals with half-cooked ingredients that are harmful to your health. Work in batches if needed and avoid overcrowding as much as possible.

- When cooking greasy meals with your air fryer, you may sometimes notice that a good amount of harmful smoke is shooting out from the air fryer! This smoke causes breathing difficulty for some. A quick way to solve this is to have a little bit of water handy. If you see that smoke is coming out, take out the cooking basket and add about 2 tablespoons of water to the cooking basket. It will gradually stop the smoke formation and allow the air fryer to cook your meal properly.

HOW TO GET THE BEST RESULTS USING OUR RECIPES!

If you are an experienced chef, chances are that you already know about the tips that I am going to share below, and have already started to modify the recipes in this book to your liking, however, for those of you who are completely new to air frying, the following tips will help get the best and most delicious results from our recipes!

· Before starting to prepare the recipe, always make sure that your air fryer is clean and free of dirt and debris. Alternatively, clean your air fryer once the cooking session is complete.

· The location of the air fryer is extremely crucial to evenly cook the ingredients, so make sure that you don't keep it in a space that blocks the air vents. Keep it in an elevated space with lots of room around it to "breath" in air and cook the meals.

· Make sure that you don't forget to pre-heat your air fryer before cooking. However, keep in mind that the air fryer pre-heats very rapidly, so pre-heating it just 2-3 minutes before cooking should be enough.

· If you are using any frozen ingredients, make sure to thaw it before adding them to your air fryer cooking basket.

· Regardless of the ingredient that you use, for example fish/poultry/meat/vegetable, always try to get the freshest one from the market, and opt for organic ones whenever you can.

· When choosing your ingredients and/or spices, always try to go for unprocessed ones - they will ensure that you are getting the most natural flavor out of your meal.

· Always try to use baking trays or dishes that are lighter in color. Extremely dark colors, such as black, will cause the tray itself to absorb more heat. This might result in uneven cooking and the lower part of your meal might remain uncooked.

· Make sure to read the recipes thoroughly before starting to cook the meal. If you find anything confusing, do a quick google search to get an idea of the process.

· Try to collect all the ingredients beforehand, however, if you are in a situation where you are unable to procure a certain ingredient, make sure to do proper research before choosing an alternative. The recipes in this book have their ingredients chosen very carefully to give you the maximum flavor - altering them might significantly alter how the dish is originally supposed to taste.

· If you ever find yourself confused with the temperatures, refer to the cooking chart below to clear up your confusion. Temperature plays a key role in air frying, and it is highly recommended that you respect the required temperatures properly.

GENERAL COOKING TIME TABLE

While all of the recipes in this book already have their temperatures and time given, it never hurts to have a reference table nearby, right? This table will greatly help you if you decide to go out and experiment with ingredients on your own!

MEAT

	Cooking Temperature (F)	Cooking Time (Minutes)
Bacon	350	8-12
Chicken (Whole)	350	45-65
Chicken Breasts (Bone-In)	375	25-35
Chicken Breasts (Boneless)	350	15-20
Chicken Tenders	350	8-12
Chicken Thighs (Bone-In)	400	15-22
Chicken Thighs (Boneless)	375	16-21
Chicken Wings	375	18-28
Lamb (Leg)	375	18-28
Lamb (Rack)	375	10-17
NY Strip Steak	400	8-14
Pork Chops	350	10-15
Pork Tenderloin	375	15-25
Ribeye/T-Bone	400	15-25

GROUND MEAT

	Cooking Temperature (F)	Cooking Time (Minutes)
Burger Patties (1/4 lb)	350	8-12
Meatballs	350	45-65
Sausages (raw)	375	25-35
Sausages (cooked)	350	15-20

CHOPPED SEAFOOD/MEAT

	Cooking Temperature (F)	Cooking Time (Minutes)
Chicken	400	8-15
Pork	375	8-12
Steak	400	8-12
Salmon	400	6-12
Tilapia	350	6-10

OTHERS

	Cooking Temperature (F)	Cooking Time (Minutes)
Banana (sliced)	375	6-8
Chickpeas	400	12-17
Tofu (cubed)	375	12-17
Tortilla chips	350	3-8
Pizza (personal size)	375	7-12

FROZEN FOOD

	Cooking Temperature (F)	Cooking Time (Minutes)
Chicken Tenders (breaded and pre-cooked)	375	14-18
Dumplings/Potstickers	400	6-10
Egg Rolls	350	8-14
Fish Sticks	400	8-12
French Fries	400	14-17
Hash Browns	325	6-9
Mini Pizzas	375	8-15
Mozarella Sticks	375	7-10
Onion Rings	400	8-10
Tater Tots	400	10-15

VEGETABLES

	Cooking Temperature (F)	Cooking Time (Minutes)
Broccoli	400	5-9
Brussels Sprouts (halved)	375	9-16
Butternut Squash (chopped)	400	15-20
Carrots (chopped)	400	10-15
Cauliflower (whole)	350	15-20
Cauliflower (chopped)	400	10-15
Corn on the Cob	400	8-10
Eggplant	400	15-18
Green Beans	400	8-10
Kale Leaves	375	4-5
Mushrooms (Button)	375	8-13
Mushrooms (Portobellos)	350	10-12
Okra	350	12-14
Onions (sliced)	400	8-10
Parsnips (chopped)	375	10-16
Peppers (small)	400	4-8
Potatoes (whole)	400	30-45
Potatoes (chopped)	375	15-30
Sweet Potatoes (chopped)	400	8-15
Sweet Potatoes (whole)	375	30-245
Tomatoes (cherry)	350	5-8
Tomatoes (halved)	350	6-12
Zucchini (chopped)	350	8-12
Zucchini (noodles)	400	10-20

GENERAL TROUBLESHOOTING GUIDE

Despite everything, if you still find yourself in a pickle, the guide below should help you solve some of the common issues.

Problem	Solution
Air fryer not turning on/ not starting cook sequence	Ensure that the device is plugged in properly and the preparation time and temperature are set.
Food not cooked properly	Try to use smaller batches to ensure that everything is evenly fried. If this fails, increase the temperature.
Food not evenly fried	To ensure even frying, some foods might require you to shake the basket from time to time.
The basket won't slide in properly	This may happen due to the basket being overfilled or not being placed correctly in the outer basket. Make sure that you don't exceed the maximum specified limit of your basket. Also, while putting the fry basket in the outer basket, gently push it until you hear "clicks".
White smoke emitted from the fryer	This usually happens if you have used too much oil.

Chapter 2
BREAKFAST

BACON ASPARAGUS WRAP

Number of Servings: 2   *Prep Time: 15 minutes*   *Cooking Time: 20 minutes*

NUTRITIONAL VALUES
(per serving)

- Calories: 178
- Fat: 14 g
- Carbohydrates: 9 g
- Protein: 4 g
- Saturated Fat: 10 g
- Sodium: 563 mg
- Fiber: 1 g

INGREDIENTS

- 1 bunch of asparagus
- 4 slices streaky bacon
- 1 tablespoon brown sugar
- 1 and ½ tablespoons olive oil
- 1 teaspoon brown sugar
- Garlic pepper seasoning

METHOD

1. Preheat your air fryer to 400F for 8 minutes

2. Trim the asparagus to your desired length

3. Take a bowl and add oil, garlic, pepper, sugar to make a mixture

4. Coat the asparagus with the mix

5. Wrap one piece of bacon with an asparagus stalk

6. To secure the wrap poke a toothpick through

7. Place all the wraps in the basket in your air fryer

8. Cook for 8 minutes

9. Serve and enjoy!

SIMPLE BOILED EGG

Number of Servings: 6   *Prep Time: 1 minutes*   *Cooking Time: 15 minutes*

NUTRITIONAL VALUES
(per serving)

- Calories: 63
- Fat: 4 g
- Carbohydrates: <1 g
- Protein: 6 g
- Saturated Fat: 2 g
- Sodium: 230 mg
- Fiber: 2 g

INGREDIENTS

- 6 large eggs

METHOD

1. Preheat your air fryerto 300F

2. Put the eggs in a single layer in your air fryer basket carefully

3. Bake for at least 8 minutes for a slightly runny yolk or 12 to 15 minutes for a firmer yolk

4. Using tongs, remove the eggs from the air fryer carefully

5. Then take a bowl of very cold water and immediately place them in it

6. Let the eggs stand in the cold water for 5 minutes, then gently crack the shell underwater

7. After that, let the eggs stand for another minute or two, then peel and eat

8. Enjoy!

GRILLED CHEESE SANDWICH

Number of Servings: 2   *Prep Time: 5 minutes*   *Cooking Time: 7 minutes*

NUTRITIONAL VALUES
(per serving)

- Calories: 400
- Carbohydrate: 30 g
- Protein: 14 g
- Fat: 23 g
- Saturated Fat: 2 g
- Sodium: 670 mg
- Fiber: 2 g

INGREDIENTS

- 2 bread slices
- 2 cheese slices
- 2 teaspoons butter

METHOD

1. Pre-heat your air fryer to a temperature of 350F

2. Cut the bread slices carefully

3. Place a cheese slice on the unbuttered side of bread

4. Keep repeating until your breads are prepared

5. Place the prepared bread in your air fryer cooking basket

6. Cook for 10 minutes (making sure to flip once after 5 minutes)

7. Enjoy!

BERRIES AND BREAD DELIGHT

Number of Servings: 2　　　　*Prep Time: 5 minutes*　　　　*Cooking Time: 10 minutes*

NUTRITIONAL VALUES
(per serving)

- Calories: 90
- Fat: 2 g
- Carbohydrates: 18 g
- Protein: 4 g
- Saturated Fat: 1 g
- Sodium: 280 mg
- Fiber: 1 g

INGREDIENTS

- 2 large whole eggs
- 1 teaspoon vanilla extract
- 2 thick slices bread
- A squeeze of honey
- 2 teaspoons low-fat Greek yoghurt
- 1 portion of butter

METHOD

1. Pre-heat your air fryer to a temperature of 356F

2. Take a bowl and beat your eggs well

3. Add vanilla to the egg and mix well

4. Take a slice of bread and carefully butter both sides of the bread

5. Soak the bread in your egg mix until it has properly absorbed the mix

6. Take out the air fryer cooking basket and place the bread on top

7. Allow them to cook for about 6 minutes, making sure to give the bread a turn halfway through

8. Once done, serve the bread with some yogurt, berries and honey

ORIGINAL FRENCH TOAST

Number of Servings: 4   *Prep Time: 5 minutes*   *Cooking Time: 10 minutes*

NUTRITIONAL VALUES
(per serving)

- Calories: 124
- Fat: 1 g
- Carbohydrates: 25 g
- Protein: 8 g
- Saturated Fat: 0.2 g
- Sodium: 504 mg
- Fiber: 2 g

INGREDIENTS

- 4 bread slices
- 2 tablespoons butter
- 2 beaten eggs
- Salt and pepper as needed
- Cinnamon as needed
- Nutmeg as needed
- Ground clove spices, as needed
- Icing sugar for garnish
- Maple syrup for garnish

METHOD

1. Preheat your oven to 360F

2. Take a bowl and add eggs, beat well

3. Season egg mix with cinnamon and nutmeg

4. Add ground cloves and mix

5. Take bread slices and butter both sides

6. Dredge them in the mixture

7. Arrange in your air fryer cooking basket and cook for 6 minutes

8. Serve and enjoy!

FRESH POTATO PANCAKES

Number of Servings: 2   *Prep Time: 10 minutes*   *Cooking Time: 24 minutes*

NUTRITIONAL VALUES
(per serving)

- Calories: 248
- Fat: 11 g
- Carbohydrates: 33 g
- Protein: 6 g
- Saturated Fat: 3 g
- Sodium: 470 mg
- Fiber: 1 g

INGREDIENTS

- 4 medium potatoes, peeled and cleaned
- 1 medium onion, chopped
- 1 beaten egg
- ¼ cup milk
- 2 tablespoons unsalted butter
- ½ teaspoon garlic powder
- ¼ teaspoon salt
- 3 tablespoons all-purpose flour
- Pepper as needed

METHOD

1. Peel your potatoes and shred them up

2. Soak the shredded potatoes under cold water to remove starch

3. Drain the potatoes

4. Take a bowl and add eggs, milk, butter, garlic powder, saltand pepper

5. Add in flour

6. Mix well

7. Add the shredded potatoes

8. Preheat your air fryer to a temperature of 390F

9. Add ¼ cup of the potato pancake batter to your cooking basket and cook for 12 minutes until a golden-brown texture is seen

10. Enjoy!

BACON MUFFIN

Number of Servings: 1   Prep Time: 10 minutes   Cooking Time: 7 minutes

NUTRITIONAL VALUES
(per serving)

- Calories: 500
- Fat: 48 g
- Carbohydrates: 38 g
- Protein: 24 g
- Saturated Fat: 1 g
- Sodium: 552 mg
- Fiber: 1 g

INGREDIENTS

- 1 whole egg
- 2 rashers streaky bacon
- 1 English muffin
- Salt and pepper to taste

METHOD

1. Preheat your air fryer to 200F

2. Take an ovenproof bowl and crack in the egg

3. Take air fryer cooking basket and add bacon, egg and muffin into fryer

4. Cook for 7 minutes

5. Assemble muffin by packing bacon and egg on top of English muffin

6. Serve and enjoy!

CHEESY MORNING MAC

Number of Servings: 1   *Prep Time: 10 minutes*   *Cooking Time: 10 minutes*

NUTRITIONAL VALUES
(per serving)

- Calories: 153
- Fat: 11 g
- Carbohydrates: 14 g
- Protein: 6 g
- Saturated Fat: 6 g
- Sodium: 147 mg
- Fiber: 1 g

INGREDIENTS

- 1 cup elbow macaroni
- ½ cup broccoli
- ½ cup warmed milk
- 1 and ½ cups cheddar cheese, grated
- Salt and pepper to taste
- 1 tablespoon parmesan cheese, grated

METHOD

1. Pre-heat your fryer to 400F

2. Take a pot and add water, allow it to boil

3. Add macaroni and veggies and broil for about 10 minutes until the mixture is Al Dente

4. Drain the pasta and vegetables

5. Toss the pasta and veggies with cheese

6. Season with some pepper and salt and transfer the mixture to your fryer

7. Sprinkle some more parmesan on top and cook for about 15 minutes

8. Allow it to cool for about 10 minutes, once done

9. Enjoy!

CHEESY OMELET

Number of Servings: 2   *Prep Time: 10 minutes*   *Cooking Time: 10 minutes*

NUTRITIONAL VALUES
(per serving)

- Calories: 396
- Fat: 23 g
- Carbohydrates: 1 g
- Protein: 27 g
- Saturated Fat: 7 g
- Sodium: 0 mg
- Fiber: 1 g

INGREDIENTS

- 2 whole eggs
- Salt and pepper to taste
- 1 tablespoon cheddar cheese
- 1 onion, sliced
- 1 red pepper, sliced
- 2 teaspoons coconut aminos

METHOD

1. Preheat your air fryer up to 340F

2. Clean and chop onion and red pepper

3. Take a plate and cover with 2 teaspoons coconut aminos

4. Transfer into the air fryer and cook for 8 minutes

5. Beat eggs and add pepper with salt

6. Pour the egg mixture on the onions and cook the mix in your air fryer for 3 minutes more

7. Add cheddar cheese and bake for 2 minutes more

8. Serve with fresh basil leaves

9. Enjoy!

HAM, ONION AND CHEESE QUICHE

Number of Servings: 2   *Prep Time: 10 minutes*   *Cooking Time: 15 minutes*

NUTRITIONAL VALUES
(per serving)

- Calories: 80
- Fat: 5 g
- Carbohydrates: 0 g
- Protein: 7 g
- Saturated Fat: 1 g
- Sodium: 0 mg
- Fiber: 0 g

INGREDIENTS

- 5 whole eggs
- 2 and ¼ ounces ham
- 1 cup milk
- 1/8 teaspoon pepper
- 1 and ½ cup Swiss cheese
- ¼ teaspoon salt
- ¼ cup Green onion
- ½ teaspoon thyme

METHOD

1. Pre-heat your Fryer to 350F

2. Crack your eggs in a bowl and beat it well

3. Add thyme, onion, salt, Swiss cheese, pepper, milk to the beaten eggs

4. Prepare your baking forms for muffins and place ham slices in each baking form

5. Cover the ham with egg mixture

6. Transfer to air fryer and bake for 15 minutes

7. Serve and enjoy!

HERBED UP ROASTED MUSHROOMS

Number of Servings: 4   Prep Time: 10 minutes   Cooking Time: 12-15 minutes

NUTRITIONAL VALUES
(per serving)

- Calories: 2198
- Fat: 18 g
- Carbohydrates: 6 g
- Protein: 6 g
- Saturated Fat: 2 g
- Sodium: 289 mg
- Fiber: 2 g

INGREDIENTS

- 1 cup walnuts, soaked
- 1 garlic clove, chopped
- 1 tablespoon lemon juice
- ½ teaspoon salt
- ¼ teaspoon pepper
- ¼ cup dill, chopped
- ¼ cup fresh parsley, chopped
- ¼ teaspoon cayenne pepper
- 10 mushrooms, stems removed

METHOD

1. Preheat your air fryer to 320F

2. Take a baking dish and line with parchment paper

3. Add nuts, clove, juice, salt to a food processor and blend until smooth

4. Add cayenne, dill, parsley and blend more

5. Stuff mushroom with the mix

6. Transfer them to your baking dish

7. Transfer baking dish to air fryer cooking basket

8. Cook for 12-15 minutes until soft

9. Serve and enjoy!

MILKY SCRAMBLED EGGS

Number of Servings: 2   *Prep Time: 10 minutes*   *Cooking Time: 9 minutes*

NUTRITIONAL VALUES
(per serving)

- Calories: 351
- Fat: 22 g
- Carbohydrates: 23 g
- Protein: 27 g
- Saturated Fat: 0 g
- Sodium: 0 mg
- Fiber: 5 g

INGREDIENTS

- 1 tablespoon butter
- 4 eggs
- ¾ cup milk
- Ground black pepper and salt to taste
- 8 halved grape tomatoes
- ½ cup grated Parmesan cheese

METHOD

1. Preheat the air fryer to 360F and grease the air fryer pan with butter

2. Whisk together eggs with milk, salt, and black pepper in a bowl

3. Transfer the egg mixture into the prepared pan and place in the air fryer

4. Cook for about 6 minutes and stir in the grape tomatoes and cheese

5. Cook for about 3 minutes and serve warm

FRESH FETA QUICHE

Number of Servings: 4   *Prep Time: 10 minutes*   *Cook Time: 12-15 minutes*

NUTRITIONAL VALUES
(per serving)

- Calories: 2198
- Fat: 18 g
- Carbohydrates: 6 g
- Protein: 6 g
- Saturated Fat: 2 g
- Sodium: 289 mg
- Fiber: 2 g

INGREDIENTS

- 1 cup walnuts, soaked
- 1 garlic clove, chopped
- 1 tablespoon lemon juice
- ½ teaspoon salt
- ¼ teaspoon pepper
- ¼ cup dill, chopped
- ¼ cup fresh parsley, chopped
- ¼ teaspoon cayenne pepper
- 10 mushrooms, stems removed

METHOD

1. Preheat your air fryer to 320F

2. Take a baking dish and line with parchment paper

3. Add nuts, clove, juice, salt to a food processor and blend until smooth

4. Add cayenne, dill, parsley and blend more

5. Stuff mushroom with the mix

6. Transfer them to your baking dish

7. Transfer baking dish to air fryer cooking basket

8. Cook for 12-15 minutes until soft

9. Serve and enjoy!

Chapter 3
APPETIZER & SNACKS

DELICIOUS SPICED UP PEANUTS

Number of Servings: 2   *Prep Time: 10 minutes*   *Cooking Time: 10 minutes*

NUTRITIONAL VALUES
(per serving)

- Calories: 157
- Fat: 7 g
- Carbohydrates: 2 g
- Protein: 22 g
- Saturated Fat: 2 g
- Sodium: 79 mg
- Fiber: 3 g

INGREDIENTS

- 2 teaspoons rice flour
- 2 teaspoons flour
- 2 cups of raw peanuts
- Pinch of baking soda
- ½ teaspoon turmeric powder
- Salt and pepper, to taste

METHOD

1. Preheat your air fryer to 390F

2. Take a bowl and mix both flours, red chili, pepper, turmeric, salt, and baking soda

3. Add the peanuts and toss them well in the mixture until fully coated

4. Transfer prepared peanuts to the air fryer cooking basket

5. Cook for 10 minutes

6. Serve and enjoy once done!

CRUNCHY ONION RINGS

Number of Servings: 2   *Prep Time: 10 minutes*   *Cooking Time: 10 minutes*

NUTRITIONAL VALUES
(per serving)

- Calories: 497
- Fat: 13 g
- Carbohydrates: 56 g
- Protein: 30 g
- Saturated Fat: 3 g
- Sodium: 145 mg
- Fiber: 5 g

INGREDIENTS

- ¼ teaspoon salt
- 1 whole egg
- ¾ cup milk
- 1 tablespoon baking powder
- ¾ cup breadcrumbs
- 1 large onion
- 1 cup flour
- 1 teaspoon paprika

METHOD

1. Preheat your air fryer to 340F

2. Take a bowl and whisk in eggs, milk, salt, flour, paprika together and mix well

3. Slice onion and separate them into rings

4. Grease your air fryer cooking basket with cooking spray

5. Dip onion rings into the batter and coat them with breadcrumbs

6. Transfer to your air fryer cooking basket, cook for 10 minutes

7. Serve and enjoy!

ROASTED BELL PEPPER

Number of Servings: 4   Prep Time: 10 minutes   Cooking Time: 5 minutes

NUTRITIONAL VALUES
(per serving)

- Calories: 59
- Fat: 6 g
- Carbohydrates: 6 g
- Protein: 2 g
- Saturated Fat: 2 g
- Sodium: 0 mg
- Fiber: 1g

INGREDIENTS

- 4 bell peppers
- 1 teaspoon olive oil
- 1 tablespoon lemon juice
- ¼ teaspoon garlic, minced
- 1 teaspoon parsley, chopped
- 1 pinch sea salt
- Pinch of pepper

METHOD

1. Preheat your air fryer to 390F in "AIR FRY" mode

2. Add bell pepper in the air fryer

3. Drizzle it with the olive oil and air fry for 5 minutes

4. Take a serving plate and transfer it

5. Take a small bowl and add garlic, parsley, lemon juice, salt and pepper

6. Mix them well and drizzle the mixture over the peppers

7. Serve and enjoy!

PORTOBELLO MUSHROOM BURGERS

Number of Servings: 2   *Prep Time: 10 minutes*   *Cooking Time: 15-20 minutes*

NUTRITIONAL VALUES
(per serving)

- Calories: 358
- Fat: 13 g
- Carbohydrates: 50 g
- Protein: 15g
- Saturated Fat: 2 g
- Sodium: 258 mg
- Fiber: 2 g

INGREDIENTS

- 2 cups portobello mushroom caps
- 1 avocado, sliced
- 1 plum tomato, sliced
- 1 cup torn lettuce
- 1 cup purslane
- ½ teaspoon cayenne
- 1 teaspoon oregano
- 2 teaspoons basil
- 3 tablespoons olive oil

METHOD

1. Remove mushroom stems and cut off ½ inch slices from top

2. Take a bowl and mix in onion powder, cayenne, oregano, olive oil, and basil

3. Cover air fryer basket with a baking sheet, brush grape seed oil

4. Put caps on baking sheet

5. Pour mixture on top and let them sit for 10 minutes

6. Preheat your air fryer 400 F and transfer to fryer, bake for 8 minutes, flip and bake for 8 minutes more

7. Lay caps on serving dish, layer sliced avocado, tomato, lettuce, purslane

8. Cover with another mushroom cap

9. Serve and enjoy!

PICKLE CHIPS

Number of Servings: 4   Prep Time: 30 minutes   Cooking Time: 20 minutes

NUTRITIONAL VALUES
(per serving)

- Calories: 59
- Fat: 0.5 g
- Carbohydrates: 11.5 g
- Protein: 2.5 g
- Saturated Fat: 0 g
- Sodium: 0 mg
- Fiber: 6 g

INGREDIENTS

- 24 hamburger dill pickle chips
- 1/3 cup whole-wheat panko breadcrumbs
- ¼ teaspoon garlic powder
- ¼ cup (2 large) egg white or fat-free liquid egg
- Dash cayenne pepper
- ¼ teaspoon onion powder
- Ketchup. to dip
- Dash of salt and black pepper

METHOD

1. Preheat your air fryer to 375F for 8 minutes

2. Spray oil in the fryer basket

3. Take a bowl and mix breadcrumbs with seasoning into it

4. Blot pickle chips dry

5. Transfer them into a small - medium bowl

6. Coat with egg whites to both sides

7. Remove the excess eggs and then coat with seasoning

8. Bake for 10 minutes

9. Bake 10 minutes more to make it crispy

10. Serve and enjoy!

LOW-CARB FISH NUGGETS

Number of Servings: 2   *Prep Time: 10 minutes*   *Cooking Time: 15-20 minutes*

NUTRITIONAL VALUES
(per serving)

· Calories: 196
· Fat: 14 g
· Carbohydrates: 6 g
· Protein: 14 g
· Saturated Fat: 2 g
· Sodium: 467 mg
· Fiber: 1 g

INGREDIENTS

· 1 pound fresh cod
· 2 tablespoons olive oil
· ½ cup almond flour
· 2 large finely beaten eggs
· 1-2 cups almond meal
· Salt as needed

METHOD

1. Preheat your air fryer to 388F

2. Take a food processor and add olive oil, almond meal, salt and blend

3. Take three bowls and add almond flour, almond meal, beaten eggs individually

4. Take cod and cut into slices of 1-inch thickness and 2-inch length

5. Dredge slices in flour, eggs and in crumbs

6. Transfer nuggets to air fryer cooking basket and cook for 10 minutes until golden

7. Serve and enjoy!

INGENIOUS SALTY PARSNIPS

Number of Servings: 2   *Prep Time: 5 minutes*   *Cooking Time: 15 minutes*

NUTRITIONAL VALUES
(per serving)

· Calories: 228
· Carbohydrate: 15 g
· Protein: 4 g
· Fat: 17 g
· Saturated Fat: 10 g
· Sodium: 685 mg
· Fiber: 3 g

INGREDIENTS

· 3 Parsnips
· 2-ounce almond flour
· 1 cup of water
· 2 tablespoon olive oil
· Salt as needed

METHOD

1. Peel the parsnips and slice them up into French fry shapes

2. Take a bowl and add water, salt, olive oil and almond flour

3. Mix well

4. Add the parsnips and coat them evenly

5. Pre-heat your fryer to 400F

6. Add parsnips to the fryer and cook for 15 minutes

7. Serve and enjoy!

DELICIOUS SAUSAGE BALLS

Number of Servings: 4   *Prep Time: 10 minutes*   *Cooking Time: 15-20 minutes*

NUTRITIONAL VALUES
(per serving)

- Calories: 65
- Fat: 2 g
- Carbohydrates: 6 g
- Protein: 5 g
- Saturated Fat: 1 g
- Sodium: 268 mg
- Fiber: 2 g

INGREDIENTS

- 3 and ½ ounces sausage meat
- 1 teaspoon sage
- 3 tablespoons almond meal
- 1 onion, diced
- ¼ teaspoon salt
- ½ teaspoon garlic powder
- 1/8 teaspoon black pepper

METHOD

1. Take a bowl and mix all the ingredients

2. Take 2-3 tablespoons mixture and make a ball

3. Repeat the process for rest of the mixture

4. Preheat your air fryer at 350 F, transfer to your cooking basket

5. Cook for 15-20 minutes

PAPRIKA AND BACON SHRIMP

Number of Servings: 2   Prep Time: 10 minutes   Cooking Time: 10 minutes

NUTRITIONAL VALUES
(per serving)

- Calories: 282
- Fat: 22 g
- Carbohydrates: 3 g
- Protein: 18 g
- Saturated Fat: 2 g
- Sodium: 269 mg
- Fiber: 1 g

INGREDIENTS

- 1 and ¼ pounds, shrimp, peeled and deveined
- 1 teaspoon paprika
- ½ teaspoon ground pepper
- ½ teaspoon red pepper flakes, crushed
- 1 tablespoon salt
- 1 teaspoon chili powder
- 1 tablespoon shallot powder
- ¼ teaspoon cumin powder
- 1 and ¼ pounds bacon slices

METHOD

1. Preheat your air fry at 360F

2. Toss shrimps with seasoning until they are coated well

3. Wrap slices of bacon around shrimp, secure with a toothpick, repeat with remaining ingredients

4. Let them chill for 30 minutes

5. Transfer to airfryer and cook for 7-8 minutes, work in batches if needed

6. Serve and enjoy!

HEARTY JALAPENO POPPERS

Number of Servings: 5   *Prep Time: 10 minutes*   *Cooking Time: 10 minutes*

NUTRITIONAL VALUES
(per serving)

- Calories: 65
- Fat: 2 g
- Carbohydrates: 6 g
- Protein: 5 g
- Saturated Fat: 1 g
- Sodium: 268 mg
- Fiber: 2 g

INGREDIENTS

- 10 jalapeno poppers, halved and deseeded
- 8 ounces cream cheese
- ¼ cup fresh parsley
- ¾ cup almond meal

METHOD

1. Take a bowl and mix ½ of almond meal and cashew cream

2. Add parsley and stuff the pepper with the mixture

3. Press the top gently with remaining crumbs and make an even topping

4. Transfer to air fryer cooking basket and cook for 8 minutes at 370F

5. Let it cool and enjoy!

BACON WRAPPED UP ONION RINGS

Number of Servings: 2   *Prep Time: 10 minutes*   *Cooking Time: 15 minutes*

NUTRITIONAL VALUES
(per serving)

- Calories: 444
- Fat: 41 g
- Carbohydrates: 5 g
- Protein: 13 g
- Saturated Fat: 1 g
- Sodium: 300 mg
- Fiber: 2 g

INGREDIENTS

- 1 onion, cut into ½ inch slices
- 1 teaspoon curry powder
- 1 teaspoon cayenne pepper
- Salt and pepper to taste
- 8 strips bacon
- ¼ cup spicy ketchup

METHOD

1. Preheat your air fryerto 360F

2. Transfer onion rings into a cold-water bowl and let them soak for 20 minutes, drain onion rings and pat dry using a kitchen towel

3. Sprinkle curry powder, cayenne pepper, salt, pepper over rings

4. Wrap one layer of bacon around onion, trimming any excess

5. Secure rings with toothpicks

6. Drizzle olive oil in air fryer cooking basket and add breaded onion rings

7. Cook for 15 minutes, turn them halfway through and cook for more

8. Serve and enjoy!

ONION PAKORA

Number of Servings: 3　　　*Prep Time: 10 minutes*　　　*Cooking Time: 20 minutes*

NUTRITIONAL VALUES
(per serving)

- Calories: 282
- Fat: 18 g
- Carbohydrates: 23 g
- Protein: 8 g
- Saturated Fat: 1 g
- Sodium: 353 mg
- Fiber: 4 g
-

INGREDIENTS

- 1 cup Gram Flour
- ¼ cup almond flour
- 2 teaspoons olive oil
- 4 whole onions
- 2 whole green chilies
- 1 tablespoon coriander
- ¼ teaspoon carom
- 1/8 teaspoon chili powder
- Salt as needed

METHOD

1. Slice your onion into individual slices

2. Chop the green chilies

3. Cut up the coriander into equal-sized portions

4. Take a bowl and add carom, turmeric powder, salt, and chili powder

5. Add onion, chilies, and coriander

6. Mix well

7. Add water and keep mixing until you have a dough-like consistency

8. Mix the dough and form balls

9. Pre-heat your Fryer to 392F

10. Cook for 8 minutes

11. Make sure to keep checking after every 6 minutes to ensure that they are not burnt

QUICK FRIED TOMATOES

Number of Servings: 2   Prep Time: 10 minutes   Cooking Time: 5 minutes

NUTRITIONAL VALUES
(per serving)

- Calories: 166
- Fat: 12 g
- Carbohydrates: 7 g
- Protein: 3 g
- Saturated Fat: 1 g
- Sodium: 234 mg
- Fiber: 1 g

INGREDIENTS

- 2 green tomatoes
- ¼ tablespoon Creole seasoning
- Salt and pepper to taste
- ¼ cup almond flour
- ½ cup buttermilk
- Almond meal as needed

METHOD

1. Add flour to your plate and take another plate and add buttermilk

2. Cut tomatoes and season with salt and pepper

3. Make a mix of creole seasoning and crumbs

4. Take tomato slice and cover with flour, place in buttermilk and then into crumbs

5. Repeat with all tomatoes

6. Preheat your fryer to 400F

7. Cook the tomato slices for 5 minutes

8. Serve with basil and enjoy!

Chapter 4
POULTRY

DELICIOUS CHICKEN TENDERS

Number of Servings: 3   Prep Time: 10 minutes   Cooking Time: 10 minutes

NUTRITIONAL VALUES
(per serving)

- Calories: 250
- Fat: 26 g
- Carbohydrates: 3 g
- Protein: 35 g
- Saturated Fat: 6 g
- Sodium: 933 mg
- Fiber: 1 g

INGREDIENTS

- ½ cup fresh basil
- ¼ cup fresh cilantro
- 1 tablespoon olive oil
- 1 teaspoon garlic, minced
- 1 pound chicken fillet
- 1 cup of bread crumbs

METHOD

1. Blend in fresh cilantro and basil in a blender

2. Add olive oil, bread crumbs and minced garlic, stir well

3. Cut fillet into medium tenders and add basil mixture and stir
4. Pre-heat your Fryer to 360F

5. Add tenders to air fryer and cooking basket for 9 minutes

6. Stir well

7. Once cooking is done, let them chill and serve

8. Enjoy!

LEMON PEPPER CHICKEN

Number of Servings: 1   *Prep Time: 3 minutes*   *Cooking Time: 15 minutes*

NUTRITIONAL VALUES
(per serving)

- Calories: 301
- Fat: 22 g
- Carbohydrates: 11 g
- Protein: 23 g
- Saturated Fat: 4 g
- Sodium: 339 mg
- Fiber: 1 g

INGREDIENTS

- 1 chicken breast
- 2 lemon, juiced and rind reserved
- 1 tablespoon chicken seasoning
- 1 teaspoon garlic puree
- Handful of peppercorns
- Salt and pepper to taste

METHOD

1. Preheat your fryer to 352F

2. Take a large-sized sheet of silver foil and work on top, add all of the seasonings alongside the lemon rind

3. Layout the chicken breast onto a chopping board and trim any fat and remove any little bones

4. Season each side with the pepper and salt

5. Rub the chicken seasoning on both sides well

6. Place on your silver foil sheet and rub

7. Seal it up tightly

8. Slap it with a rolling pin and flatten it

9. Place it in your fryer cooking basket and cook for 15 minutes until the center is fully cooked

10. Serve and enjoy!

COCONUT CHICKEN

Number of Servings: 4   *Prep Time: 5 minutes*   *Cooking Time: 12 minutes*

NUTRITIONAL VALUES
(per serving)

- Calories: 175
- Fat: 1 g
- Carbohydrates: 3 g
- Protein: 0 g
- Saturated Fat: 0 g
- Sodium: 120 mg
- Fiber: 1 g

INGREDIENTS

- 2 large eggs
- 2 teaspoons garlic powder
- 1 teaspoon salt
- 1/2 teaspoon ground black pepper
- ¾ cup coconut aminos
- ¾ cup shredded coconut
- 1 pound chicken tenders
- Cooking spray

METHOD

1. Preheat your fryer to 400F

2. Take a large-sized baking sheet and spray it with cooking spray

3. Take a wide dish and add garlic powder, eggs, pepper, and salt

4. Whisk well until everything is combined

5. Add the almond meal and coconut and mix well

6. Take your chicken tenders and dip them in the egg followed by dipping in the coconut mix

7. Shake off any excess

8. Transfer them to your fryer and spray the tenders with a bit of oil

9. Cook for 12-14 minutes until you have a nice golden-brown texture

10. Enjoy!

HEALTHY TURMERIC CHICKEN LIVER

Number of Servings: 2   *Prep Time: 10 minutes*   *Cooking Time: 10 minutes*

NUTRITIONAL VALUES
(per serving)

- Calories: 250
- Fat: 26 g
- Carbohydrates: 3 g
- Protein: 35 g
- Saturated Fat: 2 g
- Sodium: 324 mg
- Fiber: 1 g

INGREDIENTS

- 17 ounces chicken liver
- 2 tablespoons almond flour
- 1 tablespoon coconut oil
- ½ teaspoon salt
- ¼ teaspoon garlic, minced
- ¾ cup chicken stock

METHOD

1. Preheat your air fryer to 400F

2. Add coconut oil to air fryer cooking basket and pre-heat for 20 seconds

3. Stir well and cook for 2 minutes at 400F

4. Sprinkle chicken liver with almond flour, salt, and minced garlic

5. Add chicken stock, stir liver and cook for 5 minutes

6. Serve meat and enjoy it!

CREAMED UP ONION CHICKEN

Number of Servings: 4   Prep Time: 30 minutes   Cooking Time: 30 minutes

NUTRITIONAL VALUES
(per serving)

- Calories: 282
- Fat: 4 g
- Carbohydrates: 55 g
- Protein: 8 g
- Saturated Fat: 1 g
- Sodium: 87 mg
- Fiber: 2 g

INGREDIENTS

- 4 chicken breasts
- 1 and ½ cup onion soup mix
- 1 cup mushroom soup
- ½ cup cream

METHOD

1. Pre-heat your fryer to 400F

2. Take a frying pan and place it over a low heat

3. Add mushrooms, onion mix and cream

4. Heat the mixture for 1 minute

5. Pour the warm mixture over chicken and let it sit for 25 minutes

6. Transfer your marinade chicken to the air fryer cooking basket and cook for 30 minutes

7. Serve with the remaining cream and enjoy it!

LOVELY MUSTARD CHICKEN

Number of Servings: 4   Prep Time: 20 minutes   Cooking Time: 50 minutes

NUTRITIONAL VALUES
(per serving)

- Calories: 762
- Fat: 24 g
- Carbohydrates: 3 g
- Protein: 76 g
- Saturated Fat: 5 g
- Sodium: 320 mg
- Fiber: 1 g

INGREDIENTS

- 4 garlic cloves
- 8 chicken slices
- 1 tablespoon thyme leaves
- ½ cup dry wine vinegar
- Salt as needed
- ½ cup Dijon mustard
- 2 cups almond meal
- 2 tablespoons melted butter
- 1 tablespoon lemon zest
- 2 tablespoons olive oil

METHOD

1. Preheat your air fryer to 350F

2. Take a bowl and add garlic, salt, garlic cloves, almond meal, pepper, olive oil, melted butter, and lemon zest

3. Take another bowl and mix mustard and wine

4. Place chicken slices in the wine mixture and then in the crumb mixture

5. Transfer prepared chicken to your air fryer cooking basket and cook for 40 minutes

6. Serve and enjoy!

ORANGE HONEY CHICKEN

Number of Servings: 2   *Prep Time: 30 minutes*   *Cooking Time: 30 minutes*

NUTRITIONAL VALUES
(per serving)

- Calories: 240
- Fat: 6 g
- Carbohydrates: 21 g
- Protein: 25 g
- Saturated Fat: 2 g
- Sodium: 221 mg
- Fiber: ? g

INGREDIENTS

- 1 and ½ pounds of chicken breast
- Parsley to taste
- 1 cup coconut
- ¼ cup of coconut oil
- ¾ cup breadcrumbs
- 2 whole eggs
- ½ cup flour
- ½ teaspoon pepper
- Salt to taste 1/2 cup orange marmalade
- 1 teaspoon red pepper flakes
- ¼ cup honey
- 3 tablespoons Dijon mustard

METHOD

1. Preheat your air fryer to 400F

2. Wash your chicken thoroughly and cut it into slices

3. Take a bowl and blend in coconut, breadcrumbs, flour, salt, parsley, and pepper

4. Take another plate and add eggs

5. Take a frying pan and place it over medium heat, add coconut oil and let it heat up

6. Dredge the chicken in egg mix, flour and then with panko

7. Transfer prepared chicken to your air fryer and bake for 15 minutes

8. Take a bowl and mix in honey, marmalade, mustard and pepper flakes

9. Cover chicken with marmalade mix and cook for 5 minutes more

10. Serve and enjoy!

SESAME CHICKEN WINGS

Number of Servings: 4   *Prep Time: 6 minutes*   *Cooking Time: 20 minutes*

NUTRITIONAL VALUES
(per serving)

- Calories: 358
- Fat: 31 g
- Carbohydrates: 1 g
- Protein: 18 g
- Saturated Fat: 6 g
- Sodium: 269 mg
- Fiber: 2 g

INGREDIENTS

- 8 chicken drumsticks
- 1 tablespoon olive oil
- 1 tablespoon sesame oil
- 4 tablespoons honey
- 3 tablespoons light soy sauce
- 2 crushed garlic cloves
- 1 small knob fresh ginger, grated
- 1 small bunch coriander, chopped
- 2 teaspoons sesame seeds, toasted

METHOD

1. Take a freezer bag and add all of the ingredients except sesame and coriander

2. Seal up the bag and massage well until the drumsticks are coated well

3. Preheat your air fryer to 400F

4. Place the drumsticks into your air fryer basket and cook for 10 minutes

5. After 10 minutes, lower down the temperature to 325F and cook for 10 minutes more

6. Remove the chicken and serve with a side of rice

7. Sprinkle with some sesame and coriander seeds and enjoy!

HAM AND TURKEY SANDWICHES

Number of Servings: 4　　　　*Prep Time: 5 minutes*　　　　*Cooking Time: 10 minutes*

NUTRITIONAL VALUES
(per serving)

- Calories: 294
- Fat: 15 g
- Carbohydrates: 25 g
- Protein: 16 g
- Saturated Fat: 3 g
- Sodium: 258 mg
- Fiber: 1 g

INGREDIENTS

- 8 slices whole wheat sandwich bread
- 4 slices lean turkey ham
- 4 slices cheese
- 8 slices tomato

METHOD

1. Top up your bread slices with cheese, tomato, turkey, and ham

2. Cover it up with other bread slice

3. Pre-heat your fryer to 360F

4. Place the sandwich in your fryer and cook for 10 minutes

5. Once a golden texture is seen, enjoy!

HONEY CHICKEN DRUMSTICKS

Number of Servings: 2   *Prep Time: 6 minutes*   *Cooking Time: 15 minutes*

NUTRITIONAL VALUES
(per serving)

- Calories: 120
- Fat: 3 g
- Carbohydrates: 21 g
- Protein: 2 g
- Saturated Fat: 1 g
- Sodium: 144 mg
- Fiber: 2 g

INGREDIENTS

- 2 chicken drumsticks, skin removed
- 2 teaspoons olive oil
- 2 teaspoons honey
- ½ teaspoon garlic, minced

METHOD

1. Take a resealable bag and add garlic, olive oil, and honey

2. Add chicken and mix well, allow it to marinate for 30 minutes

3. Pre-heat your fryer to 400F

4. Transfer your chicken to the cooking basket and cook for 15 minutes

5. Enjoy!

BALSAMIC CHICKEN MEAL

Number of Servings: 2   *Prep Time: 3 hours 5 minutes*   *Cooking Time: 12 minutes*

NUTRITIONAL VALUES
(per serving)

- Calories: 421
- Fat: 7 g
- Carbohydrates: 25 g
- Protein: 30 g
- Saturated Fat: 5 g
- Sodium: 637 mg
- Fiber: 2 g

INGREDIENTS

- 2 chicken breasts
- 1 large mango, diced
- 1 medium avocado, diced
- 1 red pepper
- 5 tablespoons balsamic vinegar
- 15 teaspoons olive oil
- 4 garlic cloves
- 1 tablespoon oregano
- 1 tablespoon parsley
- Pinch of mustard powder
- Salt and pepper to taste

METHOD

1. Peel and remove the stone from your mango

2. Put ¾ of the mango on the side and dice the rest

3. Add the seasoning, alongside mango, garlic, olive oil, balsamic vinegar to your blender, and blend the whole mixture

4. Transfer the liquid to a bowl and add the chicken breast

5. Soak for 3 hours in the fridge

6. Take a pastry brush and rub the marinade on top of the chicken

7. Cook for 12 minutes at 350F in your air fryer, making sure to turn it halfway through and giving it a coating of glaze

8. Slice the avocado, remaining mango, and pepper

9. Drizzle balsamic vinegar on top and serve with a bit of sliced parsley

SPICED UP BUFFALO CHICKEN

Number of Servings: 4   *Prep Time: 10 minutes*   *Cooking Time: 30 minutes*

NUTRITIONAL VALUES
(per serving)

- Calories: 244
- Fat: 20 g
- Carbohydrates: 7 g
- Protein: 8 g
- Saturated Fat: 8 g
- Sodium: 366 mg
- Fiber: 1 g

INGREDIENTS

- 4 pounds of chicken wings
- ½ cup cayenne pepper sauce
- ½ cup of coconut oil
- 1 tablespoon Worcestershire sauce
- 1 teaspoon salt

METHOD

1. Take a mixing cup and add cayenne pepper sauce, coconut oil, Worcestershire sauce, and salt

2. Mix well and keep it on the side

3. Pat the chicken dry and transfer to your fryer

4. Cook for 25 minutes at 380F, making sure to shake the basket once

5. Increase the temperature to 400F and cook for 5 minutes more

6. Remove them and dump into a large-sized mixing bowl

7. Add the prepared sauce and toss well

8. Serve with celery sticks and enjoy!

CHICKEN CUTLET

Number of Servings: 4   *Prep Time: 10 minutes*   *Cooking Time: 25 minutes*

NUTRITIONAL VALUES
(per serving)

- Calories: 703
- Fat: 45 g
- Carbohydrates: 36 g
- Protein: 38 g
- Saturated Fat: 9 g
- Sodium: 585 mg
- Fiber: 2 g

INGREDIENTS

- ¼ cup parmesan
- 4 chicken breasts
- 1/8 teaspoon paprika
- ¼ teaspoon pepper
- 2 tablespoons panko breadcrumbs
- 1 teaspoon parsley
- ½ teaspoon garlic powder
- 1 bread loaf

METHOD

1. Preheat your air fryer to 400F

2. Take a bowl and mix in parmesan and panko

3. Mix in garlic powder, pepper, paprika

4. Mix well

5. Wash and cut your chicken breasts

6. Take a bowl and add water, take another bowl and add bread to the bowl; gently mash it

7. Cover chicken with panko mix and form chicken cutlets

8. Add bread to your chicken cutlet and transfer cutlets to air fryer

9. Cook for 25 minutes

10. Serve and enjoy!

CHEESY CHICKEN

Number of Servings: 2   Prep Time: 10 minutes   Cooking Time: 10 minutes

NUTRITIONAL VALUES
(per serving)

- Calories: 244
- Fat: 14 g
- Carbohydrates: 15 g
- Protein: 12 g
- Saturated Fat: 3 g
- Sodium: 0 mg
- Fiber: 1 g

INGREDIENTS

- 2 piece (6 ounces each) chicken breast, fat trimmed and sliced up in half
- 6 tablespoons seasoned breadcrumbs
- 2 tablespoons parmesan, grated
- 1 tablespoon melted butter
- 2 tablespoons low-fat mozzarella cheese
- ½ cup marinara sauce
- Cooking spray as needed

METHOD

1. Preheat your air fryer to 390 F for about 9 minutes

2. Take the cooking basket and spray it evenly with cooking spray

3. Take a small bowl and add breadcrumbs and parmesan cheese

4. Mix them well

5. Take another bowl and add the butter, melt it in your microwave

6. Brush the chicken pieces with the butter and dredge them into the breadcrumb mix

7. Once the fryer is ready, place 2 pieces of your prepared chicken breast and spray the top a bit of oil

8. Cook for about 6 minutes

9. Turn them over and top them up with 1 tablespoon of Marinara and 1 and a ½ tablespoon of shredded mozzarella

10. Cook for 3 minutes more until the cheese has completely melted

11. Keep the cooked breasts on the side and repeat with the remaining pieces

59

HAWAIIAN CHICKEN

Number of Servings: 4   Prep Time: 10 minutes   Cooking Time: 15 minutes

NUTRITIONAL VALUES
(per serving)

- Calories: 200
- Fat: 3 g
- Carbohydrates: 10 g
- Protein: 29 g
- Saturated Fat: 3 g
- Sodium: 0 mg
- Fiber: 1 g

INGREDIENTS

- 4 chicken breasts
- 2 garlic cloves
- ½ cup ketchup,
- ½ teaspoon ginger
- ½ cup coconut aminos
- 2 tablespoons red wine vinegar
- ½ cup pineapple juice
- 2 slices pineapple
- 2 tablespoons apple cider vinegar

METHOD

1. Preheat your air fryer to 360F

2. Take a bowl and mix in ketchup, pineapple juice, cider vinegar, ginger

3. Take frying and place it over low heat, add sauce, and let it heat up

4. Cover chicken with the aminos and vinegar pour hot sauce on top

5. Let the chicken sit for 15 minutes to marinade

6. Transfer chicken to your air fryer and bake for 15 minutes

7. Top with pineapple slices and drizzle more sauce on top

8. Serve and enjoy!

GARLICK AND BASIL CHICKEN LEGS

Number of Servings: 4   *Prep Time: 10 minutes*   *Cooking Time: 20 minutes*

NUTRITIONAL VALUES
(per serving)

- Calories: 250
- Fat: 18 g
- Carbohydrates: 2 g
- Protein: 20 g
- Saturated Fat: 1 g
- Sodium: 0 mg
- Fiber: 1 g

INGREDIENTS

- 4 chicken legs
- 4 teaspoons basil, dried
- 2 teaspoons garlic, minced
- 2 tablespoons olive oil
- 1 lemon, sliced
- Pinch of pepper and salt

METHOD

1. Preheat your air fryer to 350F

2. Brush the chicken with oil and sprinkle with rest of the ingredients

3. Transfer to air fryer cooking basket

4. Add lemon slices around the chicken legs

5. Lock lid

6. Cook for 20 minutes

7. Serve and enjoy!

AIR GRILLED TURKEY BREAST

Number of Servings: 8　　　*Prep Time: 10 minutes*　　　*Cooking Time: 40 minutes*

NUTRITIONAL VALUES
(per serving)

- Calories: 226
- Fat: 10 g
- Carbohydrates: 15 g
- Protein: 32 g
- Saturated Fat: 2 g
- Sodium: 269 mg
- Fiber: 3 g

INGREDIENTS

- 4 pounds turkey breast
- 1 tablespoon olive oil
- 2 teaspoons salt
- ½ tablespoon dry seasoning

METHOD

1. Rub 1/2 tablespoon oil all over turkey breast, season both sides generously and salt and seasoning

2. Rub remaining oil on the other side

3. Pre-heat your air fryer to 350 F, the skin side facing down

4. Turn it over and cook for 20 minutes more until the internal temperature reads 280F

5. Let it rest for about 10 minutes, serve and enjoy!

SIMPLE GARLIC HERB TURKEY BREAST

Number of Servings: 3   *Prep Time: 10 minutes*   *Cooking Time: 40 minutes*

NUTRITIONAL VALUES
(per serving)

- Calories: 624
- Fat: 39 g
- Carbohydrates: 5 g
- Protein: 63 g
- Saturated Fat: 7 g
- Sodium: 788 mg
- Fiber: 2 g

INGREDIENTS

- 2 pounds turkey breast
- Salt and pepper to taste
- 4 tablespoons butter, melted
- 3 garlic cloves, minced
- 1 teaspoon thyme chopped
- 1 teaspoon rosemary, chopped

METHOD

1. Pat the turkey breast dry and season it generously with salt and pepper

2. Take a small sized bowl and add melted butter, rosemary, thyme, and brush the mixture over your turkey breast well

3. Transfer to the air fryer cooking basket, cook at 375F for 40 minutes, until the internal temperature reads 160F, making sure to flip the meat halfway through

4. Let it sit for 5 minutes, serve and enjoy!

ORIGINAL ROASTED DUCK

Number of Servings: 2   *Prep Time: 10 minutes*   *Cooking Time: 15 minutes*

NUTRITIONAL VALUES
(per serving)

- Calories: 345
- Fat: 29 g
- Carbohydrates: 12 g
- Protein: 9 g
- Saturated Fat: 10 g
- Sodium: 304 mg
- Fiber: 2 g

INGREDIENTS

- 1 duck, halved and fully cooked
- 2-3 tablespoons orange sauce
- Salt and pepper as needed

METHOD

1. Pat the duck dry, season generously with salt and pepper

2. Preheat your air fryer to 360F

3. Transfer duck to air fryer cooking basket and cook for 12-15 minutes

4. Once done, take it out and let it rest

5. Drizzle orange sauce on top

6. Serve and enjoy!

Chapter 5
PORK, BEEF, AND LAMB

SKIRT STEAK AND CHIMICHURRI SAUCE

Number of Servings: 2   *Prep Time: 10 minutes*   *Cooking Time: 10 minutes*

NUTRITIONAL VALUES
(per serving)

- Calories: 244
- Fat: 18 g
- Carbohydrates: 7 g
- Protein: 13 g
- Saturated Fat: 2 g
- Sodium: 142 mg
- Fiber: 2 g

INGREDIENTS

- 16 ounces skirt steak
- 1 cup parsley, chopped
- ¼ cup mint, chopped
- 2 tablespoons oregano, chopped
- 3 garlic cloves, chopped
- 1 teaspoon crushed red pepper
- 1 tablespoon cumin, grounded
- 1 teaspoon cayenne pepper
- 2 teaspoons smoked paprika
- 1 teaspoon salt
- ¼ teaspoon pepper
- ¾ cup olive oil
- 3 tablespoons red wine vinegar

METHOD

1. Take a bowl and mix all of the ingredients listed after skirt steak; mix them well

2. Cut the steak into 2 pieces of 8 ounces portions

3. Take a re-sealable bag and add ¼ cup of Chimichurri alongside the steak pieces and shake them to ensure that steak is coated well

4. Let it chill in your fridge for 2-24 hours

5. Remove the steak from the fridge 30 minutes prior to cooking

6. Pre-heat your fryer to 390F

7. Transfer the steak to your fryer and cook for about until the internal temperature reaches 135F (For Rare)/ 140F (For Medium Rare)/ 155F (For Medium)/ 165F (For Well Done)

8. Garnish with 2 tablespoons of Chimichurri sauce and enjoy!

TOMATO AND BEEF MEATBALLS

Number of Servings: 3   *Prep Time: 10 minutes*   *Cooking Time: 5 minutes*

NUTRITIONAL VALUES
(per serving)

- Calories: 256
- Fat: 18 g
- Carbohydrates: 6 g
- Protein: 15 g
- Saturated Fat: 2 g
- Sodium: 309 mg
- Fiber: 2 g

INGREDIENTS

- 1 small onion, chopped
- ¾ pounds ground beef
- 1 tablespoon fresh parsley, chopped
- ½ tablespoon fresh thyme leaves, chopped
- 1 whole egg
- 3 tablespoons tomato sauce
- Salt and pepper to taste

METHOD

1. Chop onion and keep it on the side

2. Take a bowl and add listed ingredients, mix well (including onions)

3. Make 12 balls

4. Pre-heat your air fryer to 390F, transfer balls to the fryer

5. Cook for 8 minutes (in batches if needed) and transfer the balls to oven

6. Add tomato sauce and drown the balls

7. Transfer the dish to your air fryer and cook for 5 minutes at 300F

8. Stir and serve

9. Enjoy!

GARLIC LAMB CHOPS

Number of Servings: 4   Prep Time: 10 minutes   Cooking Time: 2 minutes

NUTRITIONAL VALUES
(per serving)

· Calories: 378
· Fat: 35 g
· Carbohydrates: 1 g
· Protein: 15 g
· Saturated Fat: 7 g
· Sodium: 116 mg
· Fiber: 2 g

INGREDIENTS

· 1 garlic bulb
· 3 tablespoons olive oil
· 1 tablespoon fresh oregano, chopped
· Fresh ground black pepper
· 8 lamb chops

METHOD

1. Pre-heat your air fryer to 392F

2. Take a garlic bulb and coat with olive oil

3. Roast bulb for 12 minutes in fryer

4. Take a bowl and add salt, olive oil and pepper

5. Coat lamb chops with ½ tablespoon of herb/oil mix and let it marinate for 5 minutes

6. Remove bulb from cooking tray and add lamb to the fryer, cook for 5 minutes

7. Squeeze garlic clove between your thumb and index finger over the herb oil mix, season with a salt and pepper

8. Serve the lamb chops with garlic sauce

9. Enjoy!

HERBED UP BEEF ROAST

Number of Servings: 4   *Prep Time: 10 minutes*   *Cooking Time: 12 minutes*

NUTRITIONAL VALUES
(per serving)

- Calories: 523
- Fat: 63 g
- Carbohydrates: 4 g
- Protein: 37 g
- Saturated Fat: 10 g
- Sodium: 618 mg
- Fiber: 3 g

INGREDIENTS

- 2 teaspoons olive oil
- 4 pounds top round roast beef
- 1 teaspoon salt
- ¼ teaspoon fresh ground black pepper
- 1 teaspoon dried thyme
- ½ teaspoon rosemary, chopped
- 3 pounds red potatoes, halved
- Olive oil, fresh ground black pepper and salt to taste

METHOD

1. Pre-heat your air fryer to 360F

2. Rub olive oil all over the beef

3. Take a bowl and add rosemary, thyme, salt and pepper

4. Mix well

5. Season the beef with the mixture and transfer the meat to your fryer

6. Cook for 20 minutes

7. Add potatoes alongside some pepper and oil

8. Turn the roast alongside and add the potatoes to the basket

9. Cook for 20 minutes

10. Make sure to rotate the mixture from time to time

11. Cook until you have reached your desired temperature (130F for Rare, 140F for Medium and 160F for Well Done)

12. Once done, allow the meat to cool for 10 minutes

13. Pre-heat your air fryer to 400F and keep cooking the potatoes for 10 minutes

14. Serve the beef with the potatoes and enjoy!

JUICY TEXAS RIBEYE

Number of Servings: 2   *Prep Time: 10 minutes*   *Cooking Time: 14 minutes*

NUTRITIONAL VALUES
(per serving)

- Calories: 305
- Fat: 24 g
- Carbohydrates: 2 g
- Protein: 21 g
- Saturated Fat: 2 g
- Sodium: 563 mg
- Fiber: 2 g

INGREDIENTS

- 2 pounds rib eye steak
- 1 tablespoon olive oil
- Salt and pepper to taste

METHOD

1. Pre-heat your fryer to 350F

2. Rub oil on both sides of the steak

3. Season with salt and pepper

4. Transfer the steak to your fryer and cook for about until the internal temperature reaches 135F (For Rare)/ 140F (For Medium Rare)/ 155F (For Medium)/ 165F (For Well Done)

5. Turn them over and cook for 8 minutes more

6. Cook in batches

7. Enjoy!

DELICIOUS TACOS

Number of Servings: 10 | Prep Time: 10 minutes | Cooking Time: 12 minutes

NUTRITIONAL VALUES
(per serving)

- Calories: 110
- Fat: 2 g
- Carbohydrates: 13 g
- Protein: 10 g
- Saturated Fat: 1 g
- Sodium: 225 mg
- Fiber: 2 g

INGREDIENTS

- 1 cup ice berg lettuce, shredded
- 10 tablespoons low fat cheese blend
- 10 thin corn tortilla
- ¼ cup fresh cilantro, chopped
- ¼ cup light sour cream
- ¼ cup salsa
- ½ - 16 ounces can fat-free black beans
- 1 cup beef, cubed
- 1 tablespoon taco seasoning
- ½ cup onion, chopped

METHOD

1. Pre-heat your air fryer to 380F

2. Spray tacos gently with oil and transfer them in single layer

3. Put in air fryer for 5 minutes until edges are crispy

4. Take a non-stick pan and add cooking spray, add onion and cook for 1-2 minutes

5. Add taco seasoning, cook for 1 minute

6. Add beef, coating and seasoning

7. Cook and push to one side, add beans and salsa on other side

8. Cook until warm and then fold both sides together

9. Stir cook and add cilantro and cream; stir cook until warm

10. Put the filling in tortilla (it should make 10 pieces) and decorate with lettuce

11. Serve and enjoy!

AMERICAN CORNED BEEF

Number of Servings: 2   *Prep Time: 10 minutes*   *Cooking Time: 40 minutes*

NUTRITIONAL VALUES
(per serving)

- Calories: 320
- Fat: 22 g
- Carbohydrates: 10 g
- Protein: 22 g
- Saturated Fat: 6 g
- Sodium: 839 mg
- Fiber: 3 g

INGREDIENTS

- 2 stalks celery
- 1 tablespoon beef spice
- 4 carrots
- 12 ounces bottle beer
- 1 and ½ cups chicken broth
- 4 pounds corned beef

METHOD

1. Pre-heat your air fryer to 380F

2. Cover beef with beer and let it sit for 20 minutes

3. Chop carrots and onion

4. Take a pot and place it over high heat, boil carrots, onion, beef in chicken broth

5. Drain the boiled meat and transfer to air fryer cooking basket

6. Place vegetables on top and cover with spices

7. Bake for 30 minutes in your air fryer

8. Serve and enjoy!

TRADITIONAL AIR FRIED PORK CHOPS

Number of Servings: 3 *Prep Time: 10 minutes* *Cooking Time: 30 minutes*

NUTRITIONAL VALUES
(per serving)

- Calories: 118
- Fat: 7 g
- Carbohydrates: 3 g
- Protein: 13 g
- Saturated Fat: 6 g
- Sodium: 145 mg
- Fiber: 2 g

INGREDIENTS

- 8 pork chops
- ¼ teaspoon pepper
- ½ teaspoon salt
- 2 tablespoons olive oil
- 4 garlic cloves
- 2 tablespoon sage leaves

METHOD

1. Pre-heat your air fryer to 350F

2. Prepare the stuffing by frying two onion slices in butter over medium heat for 5 minutes; add 1 small diced apple and cook for 30 seconds

3. Let the mixture cool, add sausages and chopped sage alongside breadcrumbs; mix well

4. Cut a hole in your pork chops

5. Fill up your pork chops with stuffing mix

6. Take a bowl and mix in sage leaves, garlic cloves, olive oil, salt and pepper

7. Cover chops with marinade and let it sit for 10 minutes

8. Transfer pork chops to air fryer cooking basket and bake for 25 minutes

9. Serve and enjoy!

MACADAMIA CRUSTED LAMB RACK

Number of Servings: 3　　　*Prep Time: 10 minutes*　　　*Cooking Time: 22 minutes*

NUTRITIONAL VALUES
(per serving)

- Calories: 301
- Fat: 31 g
- Carbohydrates: 5 g
- Protein: 33 g
- Saturated Fat: 2 g
- Sodium: 475 mg
- Fiber: 2 g

INGREDIENTS

- 1 garlic clove
- 1 tablespoon olive oil
- 1 and ¼ pound rack of lamb
- Salt and pepper to taste

  Macadamia crusts
- 3 ounces unsalted macadamia crust
- 1 tablespoon almond meal
- 1 tablespoon fresh rosemary, chopped
- 1 whole egg

METHOD

1. Chop up the garlic and toss it with some olive oil to make a garlic oil mix

2. Brush the lamb rack with the prepared oil

3. Season with pepper and salt

4. Pre-heat your air fryer to a temperature of 220F

5. Chop up the macadamia nuts and add them to a bowl

6. Add almond meal and rosemary and mix them well

7. Take another bowl and whisk eggs

8. Dredge the meat into the egg mix and drain excess egg

9. Coat the lamb rack with the macadamia crust and place them into the air fryer basket

10. Cook for about 30 minutes, making sure to increase the temperature of 390F after 30 minutes

11. Cook for 5 minutes more

12. Remove the meat and allow it to cool

13. Cover with aluminum foil and let it rest for 10 minutes

14. Enjoy!

LOVELY STROGANOFF BEEF

Number of Servings: 2   *Prep Time: 10 minutes*   *Cooking Time: 10 minutes*

NUTRITIONAL VALUES
(per serving)

· Calories: 361
· Fat: 16 g
· Carbohydrates: 11 g
· Protein: 35 g
· Saturated Fat: 2 g
· Sodium: 1385 mg
· Fiber: 2 g

INGREDIENTS

· 1-pound thin steak
· 4 tablespoons butter
· 1 onion
· 1 cup sour cream
· 8 ounces mushrooms
· 4 cups beef broth

METHOD

1. Put butter to a microwave container and microwave it to melt the butter

2. Pre-heat your fryer to 400F

3. Take a bowl and add melted butter, sliced mushrooms, cream, chopped onion and beef broth

4. Transfer the steak to the mixture and let it marinade for 10 minutes

5. Transfer the steak to your fryer and cook for about ... until the internal temperature reaches 135F (For Rare)/ 140F (For Medium Rare)/ 155F (For Medium)/ 165F (For Well Done)

6. Serve and enjoy!

AIR FRIED BEEF SCHNITZEL

Number of Servings: 1   *Prep Time: 10 minutes*   *Cooking Time: 13 minutes*

NUTRITIONAL VALUES
(per serving)

- Calories: 413
- Fat: 11 g
- Carbohydrates: 43 g
- Protein: 33 g
- Saturated Fat: 2 g
- Sodium: 506 mg
- Fiber: 2 g

INGREDIENTS

- 2 tablespoons olive oil
- 2 ounces breadcrumbs
- 1 whisked egg
- 1 thin beef schnitzel
- 1 lemon

METHOD

1. Pre-heat your air fryer to 356F

2. Take a bowl and add breadcrumbs, oil and mix well

3. Keep stirring until you have a good loose texture

4. Dip schnitzel into egg and shake off any excess

5. Dredge coat schnitzel into breadcrumbs and coat them

6. Layer in fryer basket and cook for 12 minutes

7. Serve with a garnish of lemon

8. Enjoy!

MUSHROOMS MEATLOAF

Number of Servings: 4   *Prep Time: 15 minutes*   *Cooking Time: 25 minutes*

NUTRITIONAL VALUES
(per serving)

- Calories: 287
- Fat: 12 g
- Carbohydrates: 6.1 g
- Protein: 37 g
- Saturated Fat: ... g
- Sodium: ... mg
- Fiber: 1 g

INGREDIENTS

- 1 lb. lean ground beef
- 1 egg, lightly beaten
- 3 tablespoons dry bread crumbs
- 1 small onion, finely chopped
- 1 tablespoon chopped fresh thyme
- 1 teaspoon salt
- Ground black pepper to taste
- 2 mushrooms, thickly sliced
- 1 tablespoon olive oil
- 2 tablespoons tomato sauce for serving

METHOD

1. Preheat your air fryer on air fryer mode to 392F

2. Take a medium-sized bowl and add beef, salt, thyme, onion, black pepper, and breadcrumbs

3. Use a spatula to thoroughly mix all these ingredients together

4. Brush a medium sized loaf pan with olive oil and grease it liberally

5. Spread the prepared minced beef mixture in the loaf pan

6. Top this mixture with mushroom slices and press them gently into the beef mixture

7. Place this pan in the air fryer's basket and return this basket to the air fryer

8. Cook the beef meatloaf for 25 minutes at 392F on air fry mode

9. Once done, remove the meatloaf from the air fryer and place it on the serving plate

10. Brush the meatloaf with tomato sauce and cut into thick slices

11. Serve warm

HONEY DRESSED PORK RIBS

Number of Servings: 2   *Prep Time: 10 minutes*   *Cooking Time: 16 minutes*

NUTRITIONAL VALUES
(per serving)

- Calories: 296
- Fat: 22 g
- Carbohydrates: 10 g
- Protein: 15 g
- Saturated Fat: 6 g
- Sodium: 469 mg
- Fiber: 2 g

INGREDIENTS

- 1 pound pork ribs
- 1 teaspoon salt
- 1 teaspoon pepper
- 1 tablespoon sugar
- 1 teaspoon ginger juice
- 1 teaspoon five-spice powder
- 1 tablespoon teriyaki sauce
- 1 tablespoon light soy sauce
- 1 garlic clove, minced
- 2 tablespoons honey
- 1 tablespoon water
- 1 tablespoon tomato sauce

METHOD

1. Prepare marinade by mixing pepper, sugar, salt, five-spice powder, teriyaki sauce, ginger juice and mix well

2. Rub mixture all over pork and let it marinate for 2 hours

3. Pre-heat your air fryer to 350F

4. Add ribs to your air fryer and cook for 8 minutes

5. Take a mixing bowl and add soy sauce, garlic, honey, water and tomato sauce

6. Mix well

7. Stir fry the garlic in oil until fragrant

8. Transfer the air fried pork ribs to the pan with garlic and add sauce

9. Mix and enjoy!

AIR FRIED BROCCOLI PORK CHOPS

Number of Servings: 4   *Prep Time: 10 minutes*   *Cooking Time: 10 minutes*

NUTRITIONAL VALUES
(per serving)

- Calories: 483
- Fat: 30 g
- Carbohydrates: 12 g
- Protein: 40 g
- Saturated Fat: 6 g
- Sodium: 1201 mgg
- Fiber: 3 g

INGREDIENTS

- 2 garlic cloves, minced
- 2 cups broccoli florets
- 1 teaspoon salt
- ½ teaspoon garlic powder
- ½ teaspoon onion powder
- ½ teaspoon paprika
- 2 tablespoons avocado oil, divided
- 2 pork chops, 5 ounces each

METHOD

1. Pre-heat your air fryer to 350F

2. Take the cooking basket and spray it with oil

3. Drizzle 1 tablespoon oil on both sides of the pork chop

4. Season pork chops generously with onion powder, paprika, ½ teaspoon salt, garlic powder

5. Transfer prepared pork chops to air fryer cooking basket and cook for 5 minutes

6. Take a bowl and add broccoli, garlic, ½ teaspoon salt, and remaining oil; toss well

7. Open the air fryer and flip the pork chops, add broccoli to the basket

8. Cook for 5 minutes more, making sure to gently shake the basket halfway through

9. Serve and enjoy!

SPICED UP LAMB SIRLOIN STEAK

Number of Servings: 4   *Prep Time: 40 minutes*   *Cooking Time: 15 minutes*

NUTRITIONAL VALUES
(per serving)

- Calories: 182
- Fat: 7 g
- Carbohydrates: 3 g
- Protein: 24 g
- Saturated Fat: 2 g
- Sodium: 458 mg
- Fiber: 1 g

INGREDIENTS

- 1 pound boneless lamb, sirloin steak
- 1 teaspoon salt
- ½ teaspoon cayenne pepper
- ½ teaspoon ground cardamom
- 1 teaspoon cinnamon, ground
- 1 teaspoon fennel, ground
- 1 teaspoon garam masala
- 5 garlic cloves
- 4 slices ginger
- ½ onion, sliced

METHOD

1. Take a bowl and add all listed ingredients, except lamb chops

2. Pulse well using a blender/grinder until the onion is finely minced, should take about 3-4 minutes

3. Transfer lamb chops to a large sized bowl, use a knife to gently slash the meat and create cuts to allow the marinade to penetrate easily

4. Add blended spice paste to the lamb and coat it well

5. Let it soak for 30 minutes

6. Pre-heat your air fryer to 330F

7. Transfer the steak to your fryer and cook for about until the internal temperature reaches 135F (For Rare)/ 140F (For Medium Rare)/ 155F (For Medium)/ 165F (For Well Done)

8. Serve and enjoy!

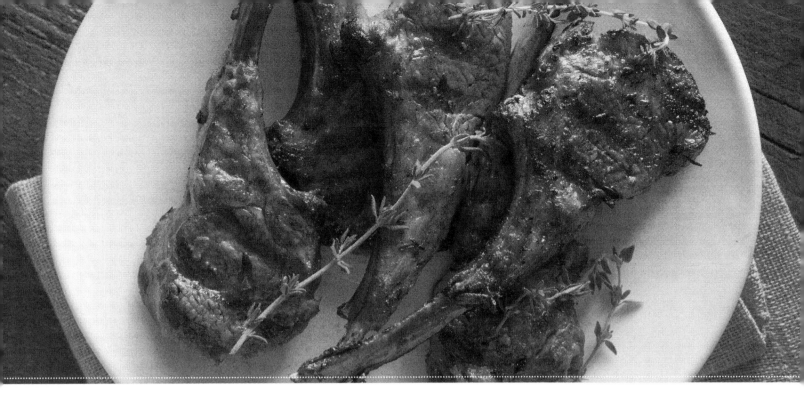

HOT ROAST LAMB RACK WITH CUMIN CRUST

Number of Servings: 2   *Prep Time: 10 minutes*   *Cooking Time: 18 minutes*

NUTRITIONAL VALUES
(per serving)

· Calories: 345
· Fat: 23 g
· Carbohydrates: 28 g
· Protein: 10 g
· Saturated Fat: 5 g
· Sodium: 107 mg
· Fiber: 2 g

INGREDIENTS

· 1 and ¾ pounds rack of lamb, frenched
· Salt and pepper to taste
· ¼ pound dry breadcrumb
· 1 teaspoon garlic, grated
· 1 teaspoon cumin seeds
· 1 teaspoon oil
· 1 teaspoon cumin, ground
· ¼ lemon, grated rind
· 1 egg, beaten

METHOD

1. Pre-heat your air fryer to 230F

2. Season your lamb rack with salt and pepper, keep it on the side

3. Take a large size bowl and add garlic, breadcrumbs, ½ teaspoon salt, ground cumin, cumin seeds, oil, and grated lemon rind

4. Take another bowl and crack an egg, beat with fork

5. Dip lamb rack into egg and coat with prepared breadcrumbs

6. Place coated lamb rack into air fryer cooking basket and cook for 25 minutes

7. Increase temperature to 392F

8. Cook for 5 minutes more

9. Remove the meat and let it sit for 10 minutes, cover with an aluminum foil

10. Slice and serve

ITALIAN PARSLEY MEATBALLS

Number of Servings: 1   *Prep Time: 10 minutes*   *Cooking Time: 10 minutes*

NUTRITIONAL VALUES
(per serving)

- Calories: 122
- Fat: 7 g
- Carbohydrates: 0.2 g
- Protein: 14 g
- Saturated Fat: 0 g
- Sodium: 1080 mg
- Fiber: 2 g

INGREDIENTS

- 1 tablespoon fresh parsley, chopped
- 1 teaspoon dried parsley
- 1 cup ground pork
- ¼ teaspoon cayenne pepper
- ½ teaspoon salt
- 1 tablespoon olive oil

METHOD

1. Blend chopped parsley, add parsley, ground pork, cayenne pepper, salt and mix well

2. Create medium sized balls

3. Spray basket with olive oil

4. Preheat your air fryer to 380F

5. Add meatball and cook for 10 minutes

6. Stir well after halfway path

7. Cook until finished

8. Serve and enjoy!

SESAME DREDGED PORK CUBES

Number of Servings: 2   *Prep Time: 10 minutes*   *Cooking Time: 15 minutes*

NUTRITIONAL VALUES
(per serving)

- Calories: 291
- Fat: 17 g
- Carbohydrates: 1.1 g
- Protein: 23 g
- Saturated Fat: 4 g
- Sodium: 1050 mg
- Fiber: 2 g

INGREDIENTS

- 1 tablespoon avocado oil
- 16 ounces of pork fillet
- 1 tablespoon sesame seeds
- 1 teaspoon ground black pepper
- 1 teaspoon Paleo Mayo

METHOD

1. Chop pork fillets into cubes sprinkle black pepper, mayo and stir

2. Add avocado oil and stir well

3. Preheat your air fryer 370F

4. Add meat to air fryer and cook for 10 minutes

5. Stir meat and add sesame seeds

6. Lower heat to 365F and cook for 5 minutes more

7. Serve and enjoy!

DELICIOUS AIR FRIED BEEF TIPS

Number of Servings: 2   *Prep Time: 10 minutes*   *Cooking Time: 12 minutes*

NUTRITIONAL VALUES
(per serving)

- Calories: 890
- Fat: 54 g
- Carbohydrates: 30 g
- Protein: 64 g
- Saturated Fat: 0 g
- Sodium: 444 mg
- Fiber: 5 g

INGREDIENTS

- 2 tablespoons coconut aminos
- 2 teaspoons rosemary, crushed
- 1 teaspoon paprika
- 2 teaspoons onion powder
- 1 teaspoon garlic powder
- 1 teaspoon pepper
- 2 teaspoons salt
- 1-pound ribeye, cut into 1 inch cubes

METHOD

1. Take a medium bowl and add cubes

2. Take another small bowl and add salt, garlic powder, pepper, onion powder, rosemary and paprika

3. Mix well

4. Sprinkle the dry seasoning all over cubes, mix well to coat everything

5. Let them sit for 5 minutes

6. Transfer to air fryer cooking basket and cook for 12 minutes, making sure to shake the basket halfway through

7. Remove from air fryer and let it cool

8. Serve and enjoy!

AWESOME AIR FRYER STEAK FAJITAS

Number of Servings: 4   *Prep Time: 10 minutes*   *Cooking Time: 17 minutes*

NUTRITIONAL VALUES
(per serving)

- Calories: 303
- Fat: 7 g
- Carbohydrates: 8 g
- Protein: 37 g
- Saturated Fat: 4 g
- Sodium: 361 mg
- Fiber: 2 g

INGREDIENTS

- 1 and ½ pounds sirloin steak
- ¼ cup pineapple juice
- Salt and pepper as needed
- 1 onion, sliced
- ½ green bell pepper, sliced
- ½ red bell pepper, sliced
- ½ teaspoon paprika, smoked
- 1 teaspoon cumin
- ½ tablespoon chili powder
- 1 tablespoon garlic, minced
- 1 tablespoon soy sauce
- 2 tablespoons olive oil

METHOD

1. Take a bowl and add paprika, cumin, chili powder, garlic, soy sauce, olive oil, lime juice, pineapple juice and mix well

2. Pour the mixture over steak and let it sit for 2-4 hours in the fridge

3. Take your air fryer cooking basket and place a foil paper in the basket, add pepper, onion

4. Spray oil and sprinkle a bit of pepper and salt

5. Transfer the steak to your fryer and cook for about until the internal temperature reaches 135F (For Rare)/ 140F (For Medium Rare)/ 155F (For Medium)/ 165F (For Well Done)

6. After the first 10 minutes, add steak pieces on top of pepper and cook for additional 7 minutes

7. Serve on tortilla, while topping with your desired fajita topping

8. Enjoy!

Chapter 6
SEAFOOD & FISH

SALMON AND DILL SAUCE

Number of Servings: 4   *Prep Time: 10 minutes*   *Cooking Time: 25 minutes*

NUTRITIONAL VALUES
(per serving)

- Calories: 199
- Fat: 8 g
- Carbohydrates: 20 g
- Protein: 23 g
- Saturated Fat: 2 g
- Sodium: 100 mg
- Fiber: 2 g

INGREDIENTS

- · 4 pieces of salmon, each of 6 ounces
- · 2 teaspoons olive oil
- · 1 pinch salt
  Dill Sauce:
- · ½ a cup of non-fat Greek yogurt
- · ½ cup sour cream
- · 1 pinch salt
- · 2 tablespoons dill, chopped

METHOD

1. Pre-heat your fryer to a temperature of 270F

2. Drizzle the cut pieces of the salmon with 1 teaspoon of olive oil

3. Season the pieces with salt

4. Take out the cooking basket and place the prepared salmon in the basket

5. Allow them to cook for about 20-23 minutes

6. Take a bowl and add sour cream, salt, chopped up dill and yogurt

7. Mix well to prepare your dill sauce

8. Serve the cooked salmon by pouring the dill sauce all over

9. Garnish with some chopped up dill and enjoy!

HEARTY FISHCAKES

Number of Servings: 2   *Prep Time: 10 minutes*   *Cooking Time: 8 minutes*

NUTRITIONAL VALUES
(per serving)

- Calories: 210
- Fat: 7 g
- Carbohydrates: 22 g
- Protein: 10 g
- Saturated Fat: 3 g
- Sodium: 300 mg
- Fiber: 2 g

INGREDIENTS

- 8 ounces salmon, cooked
- 1 and ½ ounces mashed potato
- 1 small handful capers
- 1 small handful parsley, chopped
- Zest of 1 lemon
- 1 and ¾ ounces plain flour
- Oil spray

METHOD

1. Take your Salmon and flake it well

2. Take a bowl and add flaked salmon, capers, zest dill, mashed potato

3. Mix well

4. Form the mixture into small cakes and dust them with flour

5. Place them in your fridge and chill for 60 minutes

6. Pre-heat your air fryer to a temperature of 356F, transfer prepared cakes to air fryer cooking basket

7. Cook the fish cakes for about 7 minutes until a golden texture is seen

8. Enjoy!

SPICY CAJUN SHRIMP

Number of Servings: 4   *Prep Time: 10 minutes*   *Cooking Time: 7 minutes*

NUTRITIONAL VALUES
(per serving)

- Calories: 130
- Fat: 7 g
- Carbohydrates: 16 g
- Protein: 1 g
- Saturated Fat: 2 g
- Sodium: 90 g
- Fiber: 2 g

INGREDIENTS

- 1 and ¼ pounds tighter shrimp
- ¼ teaspoon cayenne pepper
- ½ teaspoon old bay seasoning
- ¼ teaspoon smoked paprika
- 1 pinch salt
- 1 tablespoon olive oil

METHOD

1. Pre-heat your air fryer to a temperature of 390F

2. Take a mixing bowl, add the ingredients
and mix them well

3. Take your mixture and coat the shrimps with oil and spice

4. Take out your cooking basket and transfer the shrimp
to the basket

5. Cook for about 5 minutes

6. Once done, serve over some rice

CRAB CROQUETTES

Number of Servings: 3   Prep Time: 10 minutes   Cooking Time: 20 minutes

NUTRITIONAL VALUES
(per serving)

- Calories: 104
- Fat: 8 g
- Carbohydrates: 20 g
- Protein: 8 g
- Saturated Fat: 2 g
- Sodium: 177 mg
- Fiber: 2 g

INGREDIENTS

- 1 pound crab meat
- 2 egg whites, beaten
- 1 tablespoon olive oil
- ¼ cup red onion, chopped
- ¼ red bell pepper, chopped
- 2 tablespoons celery, chopped
- ¼ teaspoon tarragon, chopped
- ¼ teaspoon chives, chopped
- ¼ teaspoon parsley, chopped
- ¼ cup mayonnaise
- ¼ cup sour cream

Breading
- 3 beaten eggs
- 1 cup of flour
- 1 cup of panko bread crumbs
- 1 teaspoon of olive oil
- ½ a teaspoon of salt

METHOD

1. Take a sauté pan and place it over medium-high heat

2. Add olive oil, onion, pepper and celery

3. Stir well for about 4-5 minutes until the onions are translucent

4. Remove them and keep them on the side

5. Take a food processor and add olive oil, panko bread crumbs, salt and mix well

6. Take three bowls and add panko mix, eggs, and flour individually

7. Take a large bowl and add egg whites, crabmeat, sour cream, mayonnaise, spices and vegetables

8. Pre-heat your air fryer to 390F

9. Take the crab mix and mold it into balls or croquettes

10. Dredge them into flour, eggs and finally crumbs

11. Place the croquettes in your fryer and cook for about 8-10 minutes

12. Enjoy!

GRILLED CHEESY FISH

Number of Servings: 3   *Prep Time: 10 minutes*   *Cooking Time: 10 minutes*

NUTRITIONAL VALUES
(per serving)

- Calories: 284
- Fat: 11 g
- Carbohydrates: 5 g
- Protein: 38 g
- Saturated Fat: 4 g
- Sodium: 320 mg
- Fiber: 2 g

INGREDIENTS

- 1 bunch basil
- 2 garlic cloves
- 1 tablespoon olive oil
- 1 tablespoon olive oil
- 1 tablespoon parmesan cheese
- Salt and pepper to taste
- 2 tablespoons pine nuts
- 1 and ½ pounds white fish fillets

METHOD

1. Brush the fish fillets with oil and season with some pepper and salt

2. Pre-heat your air fryer to a temperature of 356F

3. Carefully transfer the fillets to your air fryer cooking basket

4. Cook for about 8 minutes

5. Take a small bowl and add basil, olive oil, pine nuts, garlic, parmesan cheese and blend using your hand

6. Serve this mixture with the fish

CALAMARI RINGS

Number of Servings: 2   *Prep Time: 5 minutes*   *Cooking Time: 30 minutes*

NUTRITIONAL VALUES
(per serving)

- Calories: 260
- Fat: 5 g
- Carbohydrates: 10 g
- Protein: 14 g
- Saturated Fat: 1 g
- Sodium: 180 mg
- Fiber: 1 g

INGREDIENTS

- 12 ounces frozen squid, thawed and washed
- 1 large egg, beaten
- 1 cup all-purpose flour
- 1 teaspoon ground coriander seeds
- 1 teaspoon cayenne pepper
- ½ teaspoon pepper
- ½ teaspoon salt
- Lemon wedge as needed
- Olive oil spray as needed

METHOD

1. Take a large sized mixing bowl and add flour, paprika cayenne pepper, ground pepper and salt

2. Cover the calamari rings in the egg and flour mix

3. Pre-heat your fryer to a temperature of 390F

4. Add rings to the fryer basket and grease with some oil

5. Cook for 15 minutes until they are golden brown

6. Keep repeating until the batches are done

7. Garnish with some lemon wedges and serve with sauce

8. Enjoy!

BLACK COD AND FENNEL

Number of Servings: 2　　　　*Prep Time: 10 minutes*　　　　*Cooking Time: 10 minutes*

NUTRITIONAL VALUES
(per serving)

- Calories: 269
- Fat: 1 g
- Carbohydrates: 5 g
- Protein: 32 g
- Saturated Fat: 0 g
- Sodium: 340 mg
- Fiber: 1 g

INGREDIENTS

- 2 black cod fillets
- Salt and pepper to taste
- 1 cup grapes, halved
- 1 small fennel bulb, sliced
- ½ cup pecans
- 3 cups kale, shredded
- 2 teaspoons white balsamic vinegar
- 2 tablespoons olive oil

METHOD

1. Pre-heat your air fryer to 400F

2. Season the cod fillets with salt and pepper

3. Drizzle with a bit of olive oil

4. Place the fish skin side down into your air fryer basket

5. Air fry for 10 minutes

6. Once done, remove them and make a tent with foil and allow them to rest

7. Add grapes, pecans and fennels to a bowl

8. Drizzle with some olive oil and season with pepper and salt

9. Add grapes, pecans and fennels to the basket and cook for about 5 minutes at 400F

10. Transfer the grapes, pecans and fennel to the kale

11. Dress with balsamic vinegar

12. Add olive oil

13. Season with some salt and pepper and enjoy

SOCK-EYE SALMON WITH DILL AND POTATOES

Number of Servings: 2   *Prep Time: 10 minutes*   *Cooking Time: 20 minutes*

NUTRITIONAL VALUES
(per serving)

- Calories: 224
- Fat: 11 g
- Carbohydrates: 6 g
- Protein: 14 g
- Saturated Fat: 10 g
- Sodium: 148 mg
- Fiber: 2 g

INGREDIENTS

- 2-3 fingerling potatoes, sliced
- ½ bulb fennel, sliced
- Salt and pepper to taste
- 2 pieces salmon fillets, 6 ounces each
- 8 cherry tomatoes, halved
- ¼ cup fish stock

METHOD

1. Pre-heat your air fryer to a temperature of 400F
2. Take a small sized saucepan and bring salted water to a boil
3. Add the potatoes and blanch them for 2 minutes
4. Clean and drain them dry
5. Cut out 2 large sized rectangles of parchment paper to about 13 by 15 inch sizes
6. Add the potatoes, half of the melted butter, fennel, freshly ground pepper and salt to a bowl
7. Mix well
8. Divide the vegetables between the two pieces of parchment paper
9. Sprinkle fresh dill on top
10. Place the fillet on top of the salmon on each of the veggie piles
11. Season with salt and pepper
12. Add cherry tomatoes on top
13. Drizzle butter
14. Dress with fish stock
15. Fold up the parchment squares well and seal the edges together
16. Pre-heat your air fryer to 400F
17. Cook each of the packets for 10 minutes
18. Garnish with a bit of fresh dill
19. Enjoy!

AIR FRIED CATFISH

Number of Servings: 4   *Prep Time: 10 minutes*   *Cooking Time: 20 minutes*

NUTRITIONAL VALUES
(per serving)

- Calories: 190
- Fat: 12 g
- Carbohydrates: 14 g
- Protein: 16 g
- Saturated Fat: 2 g
- Sodium: 244 mg
- Fiber: 2 g

INGREDIENTS

- 4 pieces catfish fillets
- ¼ cup seasoned fish fry
- 1 tablespoon olive oil
- 1 tablespoon parsley, chopped

METHOD

1. Pre-heat your air fryer to 400F

2. Rinse your catfish and pat it dry

3. Take a large sized re-sealable bag and add fry seasoning

4. Add catfish to the bag and seal it

5. Shake well to ensure that the fish is coated

6. Spray the fillets with a bit of olive oil

7. Place the fillets into your air fryer cooking basket and cook for 10 minutes

8. Flip and cook for 10 minutes more

9. Flip again and cook for 1-3 minutes more if you want more crispiness

10. Top with some parsley and enjoy!

GARLIC PRAWN MEAL

Number of Servings: 3   *Prep Time: 10 minutes*   *Cooking Time: 10 minutes*

NUTRITIONAL VALUES
(per serving)

- Calories: 131
- Fat: 10 g
- Carbohydrates: 4 g
- Protein: 7 g
- Saturated Fat: 1 g
- Sodium: 286 mg
- Fiber: 1 g

INGREDIENTS

- 15 fresh prawns
- 1 tablespoon olive oil
- 1 teaspoon chili powder
- 1 tablespoon black pepper
- 1 tablespoon chili sauce, Keto-Friendly
- 1 garlic clove, minced
- Salt as needed

METHOD

1. Pre-heat your air fryer to 356F

2. Wash prawns thoroughly and rinse them

3. Take a mixing bowl and add washed prawn, chili powder, oil, garlic, pepper, chili sauce and stir the mix

4. Transfer prawns to air fryer and cook for 8 minutes

5. Serve and enjoy!

CLASSIC FISH AND MANGO SALSA

Number of Servings: 2   *Prep Time: 10 minutes*   *Cooking Time: 14 minutes*

NUTRITIONAL VALUES
(per serving)

- Calories: 153
- Fat: 6 g
- Carbohydrates: 16 g
- Protein: 8 g
- Saturated Fat: 2 g
- Sodium: 36 mg
- Fiber: 2 g

INGREDIENTS

- 1 mango, ripe
- 1 and ½ teaspoon red chili paste
- 3 tablespoons coriander
- 1 lime, juiced
- 2 pounds fish fillet
- 2 ounces coconut, shredded

METHOD

1. Peel the mango and cut it up into small cubes

2. Mix the mango cubes in bowl alongside ½ a teaspoon of red chili paste, juice, zest of lime and 1 tablespoon of coriander

3. Puree the fish in food processor and mix with 1 teaspoon of salt and 1 egg

4. Add the rest of the lime zest, lime juice and red chili paste

5. Mix well alongside the remaining coriander

6. Add 2 tablespoons of coconut and green onion

7. Put the rest of the coconut on a soup plate

8. Divide the fish mix into 12 portions and shape them into cakes

9. Coat with coconut

10. Place six of the cakes in your fryer and cook for 8 minutes until they are golden brown at 352F

11. Repeat until all cakes are used up

12. Serve with mango salsa

13. Enjoy!

BROILED TILAPIA FISH

Number of Servings: 2   *Prep Time: 10 minutes*   *Cooking Time: 10 minutes*

NUTRITIONAL VALUES
(per serving)

- Calories: 177
- Fat: 10 g
- Carbohydrates: 1.2 g
- Protein: 25 g
- Saturated Fat: 2 g
- Sodium: 864 mg
- Fiber: 1 g

INGREDIENTS

- 1 pound tilapia fillets
- Old bay seasoning as needed
- Canola oil as needed
- Lemon pepper as needed
- Salt to taste
- Butter buds

METHOD

1. Pre-heat your fryer to 400F

2. Cover tilapia with oil

3. Take a bowl and mix in salt, lemon pepper, butter buds, seasoning

4. Cover your fish with the sauce

5. Bake fillets for 10 minutes

6. Serve and enjoy!

ALASKAN CRAB LEGS

Number of Servings: 4   *Prep Time: 10 minutes*   *Cooking Time: 10 minutes*

NUTRITIONAL VALUES
(per serving)

- Calories: 130
- Fat: 2 g
- Carbohydrates: 0 g
- Protein: 26 g
- Saturated Fat: 0 g
- Sodium: 1530 mg
- Fiber: 2 g

INGREDIENTS

- 3 pounds crab legs
- 2 cups Butter, melted
- 1 cup water
- ½ teaspoon salt

METHOD

1. Pre-heat your fryer to 380F

2. Cover legs with water and salt

3. Place crab legs in air fryer

4. Bake for 10 minutes

5. Melt butter and pour butter over your baked crab legs

6. Enjoy!

DELICIOUS SHRIMP SCAMPI

Number of Servings: 4   *Prep Time: 10 minutes*   *Cooking Time: 15 minutes*

NUTRITIONAL VALUES
(per serving)

- Calories: 221
- Fat: 13 g
- Carbohydrates: 2 g
- Protein: 23 g
- Saturated Fat: 4 g
- Sodium: 257 mg
- Fiber: 2 g

INGREDIENTS

- 1 pound raw shrimp
- 2 tablespoons white wine
- 1 tablespoon fresh basil, chopped
- 1 tablespoon chives, chopped
- 2 teaspoons red pepper flakes
- 1 tablespoon garlic, minced
- 1 tablespoon lemon juice
- 4 tablespoons butter

METHOD

1. Pre-heat your air fryer to 330F

2. Take a metal pan and let it heat over low heat

3. Add butter, garlic, pepper to the pan and cook for 2 minutes

4. Open fryer and add listed ingredients and cooked ones

5. Stir well

6. Cook for 5 minutes, and gently at the end

7. Sprinkle a bit of basil and serve

8. Enjoy!

HEARTY GARLIC LOBSTER TAILS

Number of Servings: 2   *Prep Time: 10 minutes*   *Cooking Time: 10 minutes*

NUTRITIONAL VALUES
(per serving)

- Calories: 450
- Fat: 24 g
- Carbohydrates: 12 g
- Protein: 9 g
- Saturated Fat: 2 g
- Sodium: 707 mg
- Fiber: 2 g

INGREDIENTS

- 4 ounces lobster tails
- 1 teaspoon garlic, minced
- 1 tablespoon butter
- Salt and pepper to taste
- ½ tablespoon lemon juice

METHOD

1. Take your food processor and add all the ingredients except lobster, blend well

2. Wash your lobster and halve them using meat knife

3. Clean the skin of lobsters

4. Cover lobsters with marinade

5. Pre-heat your fryer to 380F

6. Transfer marinated lobster to air fryer and bake for 10 minutes

7. Serve with some fresh herbs and enjoy!

Chapter 7
VEGETABLE MAINS AND SIDES

CHICKPEA AND KALE DISH

Number of Servings: 4   *Prep Time: 10 minutes*   *Cooking Time: 15 minutes*

NUTRITIONAL VALUES
(per serving)

- Calories: 220
- Fat: 9 g
- Carbohydrates: 32 g
- Protein: 8 g
- Saturated Fat: 2 g
- Sodium: 473 mg
- Fiber: 2 g

INGREDIENTS

- 2 tablespoons olive oil
- 1 tablespoon pepper
- 1 teaspoon salt
- 4 garlic cloves
- 1 can hemp milk
- 1 tablespoon ginger
- 1-pound kale
- ½ cup Roma tomatoes
- 1 can chickpeas
- 1 hot pepper

METHOD

1. Preheat your air fryer to 370F

2. Take a bowl and mix in tomatoes, pepper, ginger, milk, garlic, salt, pepper

3. Cover chickpeas with kale

4. Pour the prepared sauce on the spinach

5. Pour olive oil on top

6. Transfer the mix to your air fryer cooking basket and bake for 15 minutes

7. Serve and enjoy!

AIR FRIED AVOCADOS

Number of Servings: 1   Prep Time: 10 minutes   Cooking Time: 20 minutes

NUTRITIONAL VALUES
(per serving)

- Calories: 356
- Fat: 14 g
- Carbohydrates: 8 g
- Protein: 23 g
- Saturated Fat: 2 g
- Sodium: 304 mg
- Fiber: 3 g

INGREDIENTS

- ½ cup almond meal
- ½ teaspoon salt
- 1 Hass avocado, peeled, pitted and sliced
- Aquafaba from one bean can (bean liquid)

METHOD

1. Take a shallow bowl and add almond meal, salt

2. Pour aquafaba in another bowl, dredge avocado slices in aquafaba and then into the crumbs to get a nice coating

3. Arrange them in a single layer in your air fryer cooking basket, don't overlap

4. Cook for 10 minutes at 390F, give the basket a shake and cook for 5 minutes more

5. Serve and enjoy!

JUICY GREEN BEANS

Number of Servings: 3   *Prep Time: 10 minutes*   *Cooking Time: 10 minutes*

NUTRITIONAL VALUES
(per serving)

- Calories: 84
- Fat: 4 g
- Carbohydrates: 7 g
- Protein: 2 g
- Saturated Fat: 2 g
- Sodium: 313 mg
- Fiber: 1 g

INGREDIENTS

- 1 pound green beans, washed and de-stemmed
- 1 lemon
- Pinch of salt
- ¼ teaspoon oil

METHOD

1. Add beans to your air fryer cooking basket

2. Squeeze in a few drops of lemon

3. Season with salt and pepper

4. Drizzle olive oil on top

5. Cook for 10-12 minutes at 400F

6. Once done, serve and enjoy!

KALE AND BRAZILIAN NUT PESTO

Number of Servings: 4   *Prep Time: 10 minutes*   *Cooking Time: 20-30 minutes*

NUTRITIONAL VALUES
(per serving)

- Calories: 202
- Fat: 13 g
- Carbohydrates: 16 g
- Protein: 8 g
- Saturated Fat: 3 g
- Sodium: 358 mg
- Fiber: 3 g

INGREDIENTS

- Salt as needed
- 1 tablespoon sage
- 1 tablespoon grapeseed oil
- 1 and ½ cup butternut squash, cubed Pesto
- 2 teaspoons onion powder
- 2 tablespoons brazil nuts, chopped
- 4 tablespoons olive oil
- 2 limes, juiced
- 1 tablespoon parsley
- 2 cups kale, washed and stem removed
- 2 and ½ cups cooked quinoa

METHOD

1. Preheat your air fryer to 380F

2. Add squash to a bowl, drizzle oil and add seasoning, toss well

3. Pour squash on a baking sheet in your cooking basket, transfer to fryer and cook for 20-30 minutes until they can be easily pierced with a fork

4. Add kale, parsley, olive oil, nuts, onion powder to a food processor

5. Process well

6. Place cooked quinoa in a bowl and add pesto, mix well until pesto is evenly mixed

7. Add cooked butternut squash and toss

8. Serve and enjoy!

CRUMBLY ZUCCHINI GRATIN

Number of Servings: 3 *Prep Time: 10 minutes* *Cooking Time: 10-20 minutes*

NUTRITIONAL VALUES
(per serving)

- Calories: 367
- Fat: 28 g
- Carbohydrates: 5 g
- Protein: 4 g
- Saturated Fat: 8 g
- Sodium: 525 mg
- Fiber: 3 g

INGREDIENTS

- 3 medium zucchinis, sliced
- 2 egg whites
- ½ cup seasoned almond meal
- 2 tablespoons grated parmesan cheese
- Cooking spray as needed
- ¼ teaspoon garlic powder
- Salt and pepper to taste

METHOD

1. Pre-heat your Fryer to 425F

2. Take the air fryer cooking basket and place a cooling rack

3. Coat the rack with cooking spray

4. Take a bowl and add egg whites, beat it well and season with some pepper and salt

5. Take another bowl and add garlic powder, cheese, and almond meal

6. Take the zucchini sticks and dredge them in the egg and finally breadcrumbs

7. Transfer the zucchini to your cooking basket and spray a bit of oil

8. Bake for 20 minutes and serve with ranch sauce

9. Enjoy!

DELISH ROASTED BRUSSELS

Number of Servings: 2   Prep Time: 10 minutes   Cooking Time: 10 minutes

NUTRITIONAL VALUES
(per serving)

- Calories: 0
- Fat: 2 g
- Carbohydrates: 5 g
- Protein: 5 g
- Saturated Fat: 0 g
- Sodium: 712 mg
- Fiber: 1 g

INGREDIENTS

- 1 block Brussels sprouts
- ½ teaspoon garlic
- 2 teaspoons olive oil
- ½ teaspoon pepper
- Salt as needed

METHOD

1. Pre-heat your Fryer to 390F

2. Remove leaves off the chokes, leaving only the head

3. Wash and dry the sprouts well

4. Make a mixture of olive oil, salt and pepper with garlic

5. Cover sprouts with marinade and let them rest for 5 minutes

6. Transfer coated sprouts to air fryer and cook for 15 minutes

7. Serve and enjoy!

STUFFED BELL PEPPER PLATTER

Number of Servings: 3 *Prep Time: 10 minutes* *Cooking Time: 35 minutes*

NUTRITIONAL VALUES
(per serving)

- Calories: 154
- Fat: 10 g
- Carbohydrates: 15 g
- Protein: 2 g
- Saturated Fat: 1 g
- Sodium: 256 mg
- Fiber: 3 g

INGREDIENTS

- 4-6 bell peppers
- 2 plum tomatoes, diced
- 1 cup mushrooms, sliced
- ½ red onion, minced
- ½ white onion, minced
- 2 cups cooked wild rice
- 1 teaspoon onion powder
- 1 teaspoon oregano
- 1 teaspoon salt
- ½ teaspoon cayenne
- 2 tablespoons grapeseed oil
- 1 cup tomato sauce
- 1 and ½ cups parmesan cheese
- Springwater

METHOD

1. Preheat your air fryer to 325F

2. Cut bell peppers, remove seeds and flesh

3. Place pepper in bowl and cover with boiling water, wait for 5 minutes

4. Remove from water and place in your air fryer cooking basket

5. Add oil to a skillet on high heat, let it warm

6. Lower heat to medium and add mushroom, minced onion, and seasoning mix

7. Add cooked wild rice, diced plum tomatoes, ½ cup tomato sauce, cheese, and mix

8. Simmer for 5 minutes

9. Stuff pepper with filling mixture and spread sauce on top

10. Transfer pepper to air fryer and cook for 20-25 minutes until cooked

11. Enjoy!

BROCCOLI AND PARMESAN MEAL

Number of Servings: 2   *Prep Time: 10 minutes*   *Cooking Time: 10 minutes*

NUTRITIONAL VALUES
(per serving)

- Calories: 114
- Fat: 6 g
- Carbohydrates: 10 g
- Protein: 7 g
- Saturated Fat: 2 g
- Sodium: 626 mg
- Fiber: 1 g

INGREDIENTS

- 1 head fresh broccoli
- 1 tablespoon olive oil
- 1 lemon, juiced
- Salt and pepper to taste
- 1 ounce parmesan cheese, grated

METHOD

1. Wash broccoli thoroughly and cut them into florets

2. Add the listed ingredients to your broccoli and mix well

3. Pre-heat your fryer to 365F

4. Air fry broccoli for 20 minutes

5. Serve and enjoy!

EASY CURLY FRIES

Number of Servings: 2   *Prep Time: 10 minutes*   *Cooking Time: 15 minutes*

NUTRITIONAL VALUES
(per serving)

- Calories: 150
- Fat: 4 g
- Carbohydrates: 27 g
- Protein: 3 g
- Saturated Fat: 2 g
- Sodium: 471 mg
- Fiber: 2 g

INGREDIENTS

- 2 potatoes
- 1 tablespoon extra-virgin olive oil
- 1 teaspoon pepper
- 1 teaspoon salt
- 1 teaspoon paprika

METHOD

1. Pre-heat your air fryer to 350F

2. Wash potatoes thoroughly and pass them through a spiralizer to get curly shapes

3. Take a bowl and add potatoes to the bowl, toss and coat well with pepper, salt, oil, and paprika

4. Transfer the curly fries to air fryer cooking basket and cook for 15 minutes

5. Sprinkle more salt and paprika, serve and enjoy!

BAKED MEDITERRANEAN VEGETABLES

Number of Servings: 2   *Prep Time: 10 minutes*   *Cooking Time: 10 minutes*

NUTRITIONAL VALUES
(per serving)

- Calories: 114
- Fat: 6 g
- Carbohydrates: 10 g
- Protein: 7 g
- Saturated Fat: 2 g
- Sodium: 626 mg
- Fiber: 1 g

INGREDIENTS

- 1 head fresh broccoli
- 1 tablespoon olive oil
- 1 lemon, juiced
- Salt and pepper to taste
- 1 ounce parmesan cheese, grated

METHOD

1. Wash broccoli thoroughly and cut them into florets

2. Add the listed ingredients to your broccoli and mix well

3. Pre-heat your fryer to 365F

4. Air fry broccoli for 20 minutes

5. Serve and enjoy!

GARBANZO BEAN CURRY

Number of Servings: 2   *Prep Time: 10 minutes*   *Cooking Time: 15 minutes*

NUTRITIONAL VALUES
(per serving)

- Calories: 150
- Fat: 4 g
- Carbohydrates: 27 g
- Protein: 3 g
- Saturated Fat: 2 g
- Sodium: 471 mg
- Fiber: 2 g

INGREDIENTS

- 2 potatoes
- 1 tablespoon extra-virgin olive oil
- 1 teaspoon pepper
- 1 teaspoon salt
- 1 teaspoon paprika

METHOD

1. Pre-heat your air fryer to 350F

2. Wash potatoes thoroughly and pass them through a spiralizer to get curly shapes

3. Take a bowl and add potatoes to the bowl, toss and coat well with pepper, salt, oil, and paprika

4. Transfer the curly fries to air fryer cooking basket and cook for 15 minutes

5. Sprinkle more salt and paprika, serve and enjoy!

MUSHROOM AND SPINACH PLATTER

Number of Servings: 3   *Prep Time: 10 minutes*   *Cooking Time: 15 minutes*

NUTRITIONAL VALUES
(per serving)

- Calories: 230
- Fat: 11 g
- Carbohydrates: 18 g
- Protein: 15 g
- Saturated Fat: 3 g
- Sodium: 933 mg
- Fiber: 2 g

INGREDIENTS

- 6 mushrooms, stems removed and chopped
- 1 cup spinach, steamed, chopped
- 1 tablespoon olive oil
- ¼ teaspoon garlic powder
- ¼ teaspoon onion powder

METHOD

1. Add mushroom stems, spinach, olive oil, garlic, onion, pepper, and salt to the food processor. Pulse a few times

2. Preheat your air fryer to 330F

3. Line baking dish with parchment paper, stuff each mushroom with the mix

4. Transfer to air fryer cooking basket, cook for 12-15 minutes

5. Serve and enjoy!

STUFFED LOBSTER MUSHROOM

Number of Servings: 2   *Prep Time: 10 minutes*   *Cooking Time: 10 minutes*

NUTRITIONAL VALUES
(per serving)

- Calories: 450
- Fat: 24 g
- Carbohydrates: 12 g
- Protein: 9 g
- Saturated Fat: 2 g
- Sodium: 1070 mg
- Fiber: 2 g

INGREDIENTS

- 4 ounce lobster tails
- 1 teaspoon garlic, minced
- 1 tablespoon butter
- Salt and pepper to taste
- ½ tablespoon lemon juice

METHOD

1. Take your food processor and add all the ingredients except lobster, blend well

2. Wash your lobster and halve them using meat knife

3. Clean the skin of lobsters

4. Cover lobsters with marinade

5. Pre-heat your fryer to 380F

6. Transfer prepared lobster to air fryer and bake for 10 minutes

7. Serve with some fresh herbs and enjoy!

DELICIOUS VEGETABLE GRATIN

Number of Servings: 2   *Prep Time: 10 minutes*   *Cooking Time: 20 minutes*

NUTRITIONAL VALUES
(per serving)

- Calories: 265
- Fat: 22 g
- Carbohydrates: 6 g
- Protein: 7 g
- Saturated Fat: 2 g
- Sodium: 463 mg
- Fiber: 3 g

INGREDIENTS

- 1 eggplant, peeled and sliced
- 2 bell peppers, seeded and sliced
- 1 red onion, sliced
- 1 teaspoon fresh garlic, minced
- 4 tablespoons olive oil
- 1 teaspoon mustard
- 1 teaspoon dried oregano
- 1 teaspoon smoked paprika
- Salt and pepper to taste
- 1 tomato, sliced
- 6 ounces cashew cheese

METHOD

1. Preheat your air fryer 370F

2. Drizzle a bit of oil over a baking pan

3. Place eggplant, pepper, onion, garlic on the bottom of the baking pan

4. Add olive oil, mustard, and spices

5. Transfer to cooking basket

6. Cook for 14 minutes

7. Top with tomatoes, cheese and increase the temperature to 390F

8. Cook for 5 minutes

9. Let it cool and serve

10. Enjoy!

CRISPY LEEK STRIPS

Number of Servings: 2   *Prep Time: 10 minutes*   *Cooking Time: 18 minutes*

NUTRITIONAL VALUES
(per serving)

- Calories: 114
- Fat: 8 g
- Carbohydrates: 7 g
- Protein: 2 g
- Saturated Fat: 2 g
- Sodium: 450 mg
- Fiber: 1 g

INGREDIENTS

- ½ teaspoon porcini powder
- 1 cup almond flour
- ½ cup coconut flour
- 1 tablespoon coconut oil
- 2 medium leeks, sliced into julienne strips
- 2 large dishes with ice water
- 2 teaspoons onion powder
- Salt and pepper to taste

METHOD

1. Preheat your air fryer 390F

2. Let the leeks soak in ice water for 25 minutes, drain well

3. Place flour, salt, cayenne, pepper, onion powder, porcini powder in a bag and shake well

4. Add leeks and shake well

5. Drizzle oil over seasoned leeks and transfer them to air fryer cooking basket

6. Cook for 18 minutes, shake about halfway through

7. Enjoy!

EASY GOING PUMPKIN FRIES

Number of Servings: 2-3   *Prep Time: 25 minutes*   *Cooking Time: 10-15 minutes*

NUTRITIONAL VALUES
(per serving)

- Calories: 151
- Fat: 3 g
- Carbohydrates: 31 g
- Protein: 5 g
- Saturated Fat: 2 g
- Sodium: 413 mg
- Fiber: 2 g

INGREDIENTS

- ¼ teaspoon pepper
- ¼ teaspoon chili powder
- ¼ teaspoon ground cumin
- ¼ teaspoon garlic powder
- 1 medium pie pumpkin
- 1/8 teaspoon + ½ teaspoon salt, divided
- 2-3 teaspoons chipotle pepper, in adobo sauce
- 2 tablespoons maple syrup
- ½ cup Greek yogurt, plain

METHOD

1. Take a small sized bowl, add yogurt, chipotle pepper, maple syrup, 1/8 teaspoon salt. Let it chill in your fridge until serving time, this will be your sauce

2. Pre-heat your air fryer to 400F

3. Peel the pumpkin, cut it in half lengthwise

4. Remove seeds

5. Cut pumpkin into ½ inch strips, transfer them to a large bowl

6. Sprinkle with remaining salt, add cumin, garlic powder, chili powder, pepper

7. Toss the mixture well to coat it

8. Transfer the prepare pumpkin in batches to the air fryer cooking basket

9. Cook for about 6-8 minutes until tender, toss the mix and cook for 3-5 minutes more until crispy and browned

10. Serve with the prepared sauce, enjoy!

CAULIFLOWER HASH BROWNS

Number of Servings: 2   *Prep Time: 10 minutes*   *Cooking Time: 17 minutes*

NUTRITIONAL VALUES
(per serving)

- Calories: 155
- Fat: 11 g
- Carbohydrates: 8 g
- Protein: 5 g
- Saturated Fat: 3 g
- Sodium: 396 mg
- Fiber: 1 g

INGREDIENTS

- ½ cup vegan cheese
- 1 tablespoon cashew cheese
- 1/3 cup almond meal
- 1 and ½ yellow onion, chopped
- 5 ounces celery soup cream
- 1 tablespoon fresh cilantro
- 3 garlic cloves, minced
- 2 cups cauliflower, grated
- 1 and ½ tablespoons almond butter
- Salt and pepper to taste
- Crushed red pepper flakes to taste

METHOD

1. Preheat your air fryer to 355F

2. Take a large-sized bowl and whisk in celery cream, cashew cheese, pepper, salt and stir in cauliflower, onion, garlic, cilantro

3. Mix well

4. Scrape mix into baking dish

5. Take another bowl and add almond meal, almond butter

6. Spread mix evenly over hash brown

7. Transfer to air fryer cooking basket and cook for 17 minutes

8. Serve and enjoy!

COCONUT MILK AND ROASTED VEGGIE

Number of Servings: 3   *Prep Time: 10 minutes*   *Cooking Time: 40-50 minutes*

NUTRITIONAL VALUES
(per serving)

- Calories: 449
- Fat: 39 g
- Carbohydrates: 27 g
- Protein: 6 g
- Saturated Fat: 1 g
- Sodium: 253 mg
- Fiber: 3 g

INGREDIENTS

- Cayenne pepper, to taste
- Salt to taste
- 1 tablespoon + additional grapeseed oil
- 1 cup of coconut milk
- 1 tablespoon ginger, grated
- 1 small onion, diced
- 2 cups mixed vegetables, chopped

METHOD

1. Preheat your air fryer to 330F

2. Transfer veggies to your cooking basket, drizzle oil all over

3. Season with salt and pepper, toss well

4. Transfer to fryer and cook for 20-30 minutes until roasted

5. Take a skillet and add some oil, let it heat up

6. Add ginger and onion, cook until fragrant

7. Add coconut milk, let it boil

8. Lower heat and simmer for 30 minutes

9. Once veggies are done, pour milk mix among two bowls

10. Divide veggies evenly

11. Add more seasoning if needed

12. Serve and enjoy!

SPICY MOROCCAN CARROT ROAST

Number of Servings: 4   *Prep Time: 10 minutes*   *Cooking Time: 24 minutes*

NUTRITIONAL VALUES
(per serving)

- Calories: 99
- Fat: 7 g
- Carbohydrates: 9 g
- Protein: 9 g
- Saturated Fat: 1 g
- Sodium: 357 mg
- Fiber: 3 g

INGREDIENTS

- 1 pound carrots, peeled and sliced into diagonal pieces
- ½ teaspoon salt
- 2 tablespoon olive oil
- Fresh pepper and salt

METHOD

1. Take the carrots and peel them diagonally into slices, trying to have an even thickness

2. Take a bowl and mix all the ingredients for the Moroccan Spice Mix and prepare the mixture

3. Pre-heat your air fryer to 360F

4. Toss carrots with salt, olive oil, pepper and 1 teaspoon of the prepare mixture

5. Take your air fryer cooking basket and spread carrots evenly in a single layer

6. Cook for 7-8 minutes, shake the basket and cook for 5 minutes more

7. Serve and enjoy!

CAULIFLOWER AND BROCCOLI MIX

Number of Servings: 2   *Prep Time: 10 minutes*   *Cooking Time: 12 minutes*

NUTRITIONAL VALUES
(per serving)

- Calories: 130
- Fat: 3 g
- Carbohydrates: 9 g
- Protein: 8 g
- Saturated Fat: 1 g
- Sodium: 382 mg
- Fiber: 2 g

INGREDIENTS

- 1 cup almond meal
- ¼ cup cashew cheese
- 1 tablespoon Creole seasoning
- 2 cups cauliflower florets
- 2 cups broccoli florets
- ½ cup almond flour
- 2 flax eggs
- 1 tablespoon parsley, chopped
- Keto-Friendly marinara sauce

METHOD

1. Preheat your air fryer 400F

2. Take a large-sized bowl and add almond meal, stir in seasoning, cashew cream and stir well

3. Take another bowl and add flax egg, add almond flour in another dish

4. Dredge florets into flour, then eggs, then almond meal

5. Transfer prepared florets to your air fryer

6. Cook for 6 minutes, shake well and cook for 6 minutes more

7. Serve and enjoy once done!

TAMARI ROASTED EGGPLANT

Number of Servings: 2   *Prep Time: 10 minutes*   *Cooking Time: 13 minutes*

NUTRITIONAL VALUES
(per serving)

- Calories: 76
- Fat: 5 g
- Carbohydrates: 7 g
- Protein: 2 g
- Saturated Fat: 2 g
- Sodium: 805 mg
- Fiber: 1 g

INGREDIENTS

- Olive oil for cooking
- 1 medium eggplant, cut into ½ inch thick
- 2 and ½ tablespoons tamari
- 2 teaspoons garlic granules
- 2 teaspoons onion granules
- 4 teaspoons extra olive oil

METHOD

1. Preheat your air fryer to 392F

2. Take a large bowl and add eggplant slices, sprinkle tamari, garlic, onion, and oil; stir well

3. Transfer eggplants to air fryer cooking basket and roast for 5 minutes, remove and transfer eggplant with the remaining liquid and cook for 3 minutes more

4. Flip and cook for 5 minutes more

5. Serve and enjoy!

Chapter 8
DESSERTS

AWESOME APPLE PIE

Number of Servings: 2   *Prep Time: 5 minutes*   *Cooking Time: 20 minutes*

NUTRITIONAL VALUES
(per serving)

- Calories: 223
- Fat: 8 g
- Carbohydrates: 37 g
- Protein: 2 g
- Saturated Fat: 5 g
- Sodium: 0 mg
- Fiber: 2 g

INGREDIENTS

- 2 and ¾ ounces flour
- 5 tablespoons sugar
- 1 and ¼ ounces butter
- 3 tablespoons cinnamon
- 2 whole apples

METHOD

1. Pre-heat your Fryer to 360F

2. Take a bowl and mix in 3 tablespoons sugar, butter and flour

3. Form the pastry

4. Wash and cut apples

5. Cover apples with sugar and cinnamon

6. Lay apples on your pastry and cover with dough

7. Place pie in your fryer and cook for 20 minutes

8. Serve with sprinkles of powdered sugar and fresh mint

9. Enjoy!

MESMERIZING CHOCOLATE SOUFFLE

Number of Servings: 4   *Prep Time: 5 minutes*   *Cooking Time: 20 minutes*

NUTRITIONAL VALUES
(per serving)

- Calories: 187
- Fat: 8 g
- Carbohydrates: 28 g
- Protein: 5 g
- Saturated Fat: 2 g
- Sodium: 53 mg
- Fiber: 2 g

INGREDIENTS

- 6 tablespoons sugar
- 1 and ½ cups chocolate
- 2 egg yolks
- 4 egg whites
- 1 tablespoon heavy cream
- 1 teaspoon plain flour
- 1 teaspoon ground cinnamon
- 1 teaspoon salt

METHOD

1. Pre-heat your air fryer to a temperature of 338F

2. Take 4 ramekins and grease it up well

3. Coat the inside with 1 and ½ teaspoon of sugar

4. Add chopped up chocolate on top of a double boiler over hot, but not boiling water

5. Keep stirring until the chocolate has melted

6. You may also melt the chocolate in your microwave

7. Take a medium sized bowl and beat your egg whites, salt and 4 tablespoons of sugar

8. Keep beating it until stiff peak forms

9. Fold half of the beaten whites into your chocolate mix and keep mixing until a smooth texture is formed

10. Fold the combined mixture back into the remaining egg whites and keep mixing until the white streaks are gone

11. Divide the mix between the four different ramekins and place them in your air fryer

12. Let it cook for 15-20 minutes until it is fully puffed and strong to touch

13. Dust them with some confectioner's sugar if you want

14. Enjoy the mouthwatering soufflé!

BROWNIE AND CARAMEL SAUCE

Number of Servings: 3   *Prep Time: 5 minutes*   *Cooking Time: 15 minutes*

NUTRITIONAL VALUES
(per serving)

- Calories: 223
- Fat: 12 g
- Carbohydrates: 39 g
- Protein: 3 g
- Saturated Fat: 4 g
- Sodium: 124 mg
- Fiber: 2 g

INGREDIENTS

- 4 ounces caster sugar
- 2 tablespoons water
- ½ cup milk
- 4 ounces butter
- 2 ounces chocolate
- 6 ounces brown sugar
- 2 thoroughly beaten eggs
- 2 teaspoons vanilla essence

METHOD

1. Pre-heat your air fryer to 356F

2. Take a bowl and add butter and chocolate

3. Pour mixture into pan and place it over medium heat

4. Take a bowl and add beaten eggs, sugar, vanilla essence, raising flour and mix well

5. Take a dish and grease it

6. Pour beaten egg mixture into the dish

7. Transfer dish to the air fryer cooking basket and cook for 15 minutes

8. Take another pan and add caster sugar, heat until melted

9. Stir butter into caramel and let it melt

10. Top brownies with caramel and enjoy!

AWESOME BANANA SPLIT

Number of Servings: 4   *Prep Time: 15 minutes*   *Cooking Time: 15 minutes*

NUTRITIONAL VALUES
(per serving)

- Calories: 893
- Fat: 43 g
- Carbohydrates: 121 g
- Protein: 15 g
- Saturated Fat: 10 g
- Sodium: 177 mg
- Fiber: 2 g

INGREDIENTS

- 2 tablespoons butter
- 4 bananas
- 3 egg whites
- ½ cup corn flour
- 3 tablespoons cinnamon sugar
- 1 cup panko bread crumbs

METHOD

1. Take a saucepan and place it over medium heat
2. Add butter and allow it to melt
3. Add breadcrumbs into the butter and stir well for about 3-4 minutes
4. Once the crumbs have a golden texture and remove them from the pan
5. Place them into a bowl
6. Take a bowl and add your beaten eggs
7. Take another bowl and add the flour
8. Peel the bananas and slice them up into two
9. Roll the banana slices in the flour, eggs and then the bread crumbs
10. Once done, take out your air fryer basket and place them in the basket
11. Dust them with cinnamon sugar
12. Pre-heat the air fryer with 280 F
13. Add the bananas and cook for 10 minutes
14. Take a bowl and scoop up vanilla, strawberry and chocolate ice cream
15. Once the bananas are cooked, take out and serve with the ice cream
16. Top off with some additional nuts and whipped cream
17. Enjoy!

AIR FRIED VELVET CAKE

Number of Servings: 3   *Prep Time: 5 minutes*   *Cooking Time: 10-15 minutes*

NUTRITIONAL VALUES
(per serving)

- Calories: 249
- Fat: 5 g
- Carbohydrates: 22 g
- Protein: 31 g
- Saturated Fat: 1 g
- Sodium: 89 g
- Fiber: 2 g

INGREDIENTS

- 1 and ½ cups flour
- 1 and ½ teaspoons cocoa powder
- ¼ teaspoon salt
- 4 and ½ ounces butter
- 1 cup sugar
- 2 whole eggs
- 1 tablespoon red food coloring
- ¾ cup buttermilk
- ¾ teaspoon baking soda
- 1 teaspoon vinegar

METHOD

1. Take a bowl and add flour, salt and cocoa powder

2. Sift them well

3. Take a cake mixer bowl and add butter, sugar and vanilla. Beat the mixture well with your mixer

4. Add the eggs one at a time while beating them with the mixer

5. Add red food coloring to the batter

6. Add flour mixture to the batter as well and keep stirring it until fully incorporated

7. Add vinegar and baking soda and mix well

8. Pour the batter into muffin cups (lined with pepper cups)

9. Pre-heat your air fryer to a temperature of 320F

10. Bake the cakes for about 11 minutes

11. Remove and allow them to cool

12. Decorate if you want and enjoy!

ORIGINAL NEW YORK CHEESECAKE

Number of Servings: 6   *Prep Time: 20 minutes*   *Cooking Time: 30 minutes*

NUTRITIONAL VALUES
(per serving)

- Calories: 831
- Fat: 49 g
- Carbohydrates: 88 g
- Protein: 11 g
- Saturated Fat: 3 g
- Sodium: 465 g
- Fiber: 2 g

INGREDIENTS

- 1 and ¾ cups plain flour
- 3 and ½ ounce brown sugar
- 3 and ½ ounce butter
- 1 and ¾ ounces melted butter
- 6 and ½ cups softened cheese
- 3 large eggs
- 2 cups powdered sugar
- 3 and ¼ tablespoons quark
- 1 tablespoon vanilla essence

METHOD

1. Make the biscuit base by taking a large bowl, add flour and sugar

2. Mix well and add fat, keep mixing until you have a breadcrumb like texture

3. Combine it well and pat it into a biscuit shape and transfer them into your cooking basket

4. Grease bottom side of spring form pan with a bit of flour

5. Bake the biscuits for 15 minutes at 360 F

6. Once the biscuits are ready, break them into tiny pieces and mix with melted butter

7. Pat mixture down into bottom of spring form pan

8. Take another mixing bowl and add cheese, sugar and mix with hand mixer until you have a creamy texture

9. Crack eggs into a bowl and add essence, mix with fork

10. Stir in quark and pour the batter into prepared pan

11. Flatten the surface

12. Transfer to fryer and cook for 30 minutes at 360 F

13. Let it cool for 6 hours

14. Serve and enjoy!

CLASSIC CHOCOLATE CHIP COOKIES

Number of Servings: 6   *Prep Time: 20 minutes*   *Cooking Time: 30 minutes*

NUTRITIONAL VALUES
(per serving)

- Calories: 268
- Fat: 15 g
- Carbohydrates: 40 g
- Protein: 3 g
- Saturated Fat: 5 g
- Sodium: 117 g
- Fiber: 3 g

INGREDIENTS

- 2/3 cup flour
- ½ cup semi-sweet chocolate chips
- ½ teaspoon vanilla extract
- 1 egg yolk
- 2 tablespoons sugar
- ¼ cup unsalted butter, soft
- 1/3 cup brown sugar
- 1/8 teaspoon salt
- ¼ teaspoon baking soda
- 2/3 cup all-purpose flour

METHOD

1. Pre-heat your air fryer to 350F

2. Take your air fryer cooking basket and line them with foil

3. Take a bowl and whisk in flour, salt and baking soda

4. Take another bowl and add brown sugar, both sugars and mix well

5. Add vanilla extract and whisk until combined

6. Stir the flour mix into butter mix

7. Fold in chocolate chips

8. Scoop dough into balls and place them in your prepared basket, keeping a distance of 2 inch between the cookies

9. Cook for 5-6 minutes until crispy

10. Transfer to wire rack and let them cool

11. Repeat until whole batter is used

12. Serve and enjoy!

CONCLUSION

I sincerely convey my warmest regards and heartiest appreciation to you for buying this cookbook and taking the time to read through.

Being both the author and chef, I really hope that you were able to experiment with all of the recipes in this book and were able to find your next favorite air fryer recipe from the wide variety that I have presented here!

All of the recipes found in this book were written only after thorough self-practice and a lot of care, dedicated to the thousands of air fryer users all over the globe.

I love getting feedback from my reader. You can write me at jrose.booksauthor@gmail.com. I would also greatly appreciate it if you could review my book on Amazon. Your input would mean a lot to me!

Stay safe and stay healthy.

Go here to review the book on Amazon

INDEX

Printed in Great Britain
by Amazon